KARL BLOSSFELDT

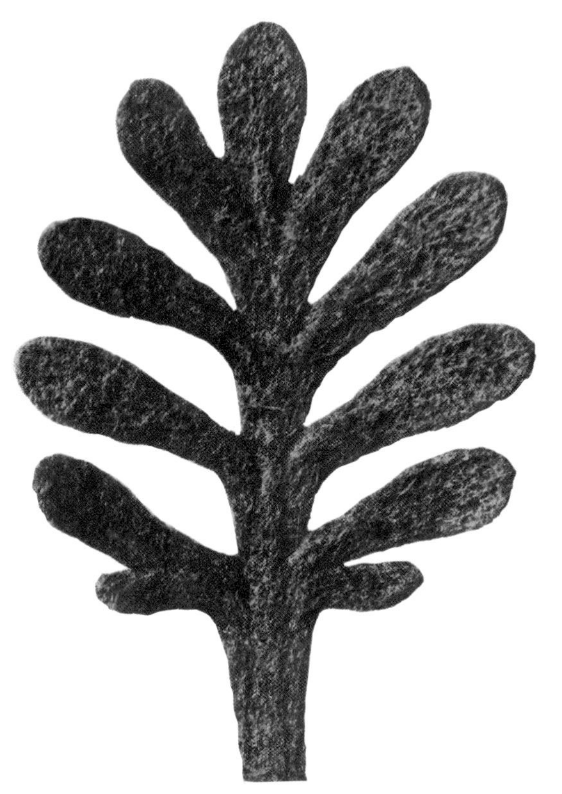

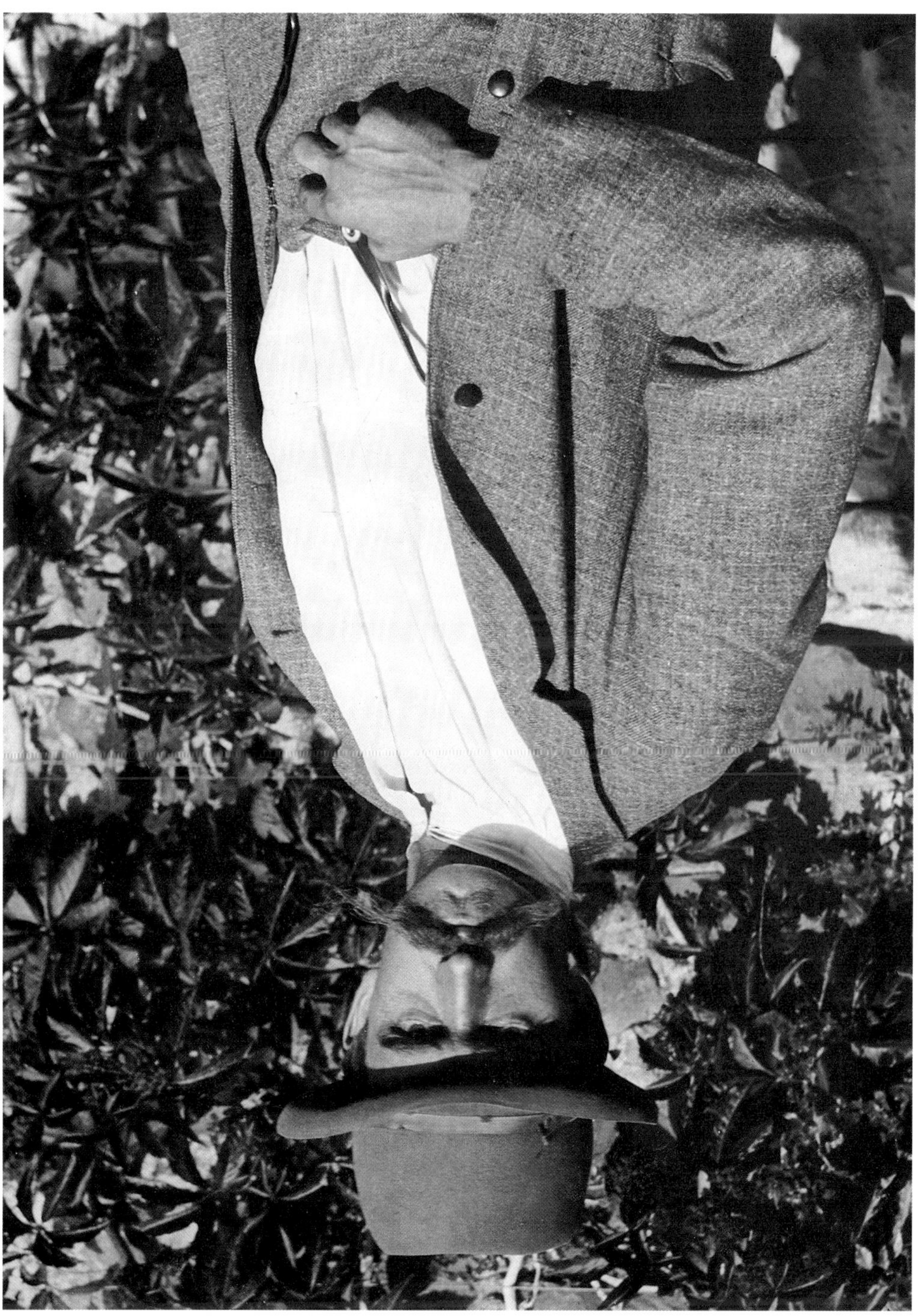

KARL BLOSSFELDT
PHOTOGRAPHS

With a text by
Rolf Sachsse

Benedikt Taschen

FRONT COVER:
Adiantum pedatum
Maiden-hair fern
Fiddleheads magnified 12 times

ILLUSTRATION PAGE 2:
Karl Blossfeldt, self-portrait, c. 1895

This book was printed on 100% chlorine-free bleached paper in accordance with the TCF standard.

Editing and design: Angelika Muthesius, Cologne
Text: Rolf Sachsse, Bonn
English translation: Angela Dunn, Leimen
Composition: Utesch Satztechnik GmbH, Hamburg
Printed by Neue Stalling GmbH & Co KG, Oldenburg

Printed in Germany
ISBN 3-8228-9319-6
GB

In his basic teaching Karl Blossfeldt simply wished to impart an awareness that the best engineering solutions for industrial design had already been anticipated in nature.

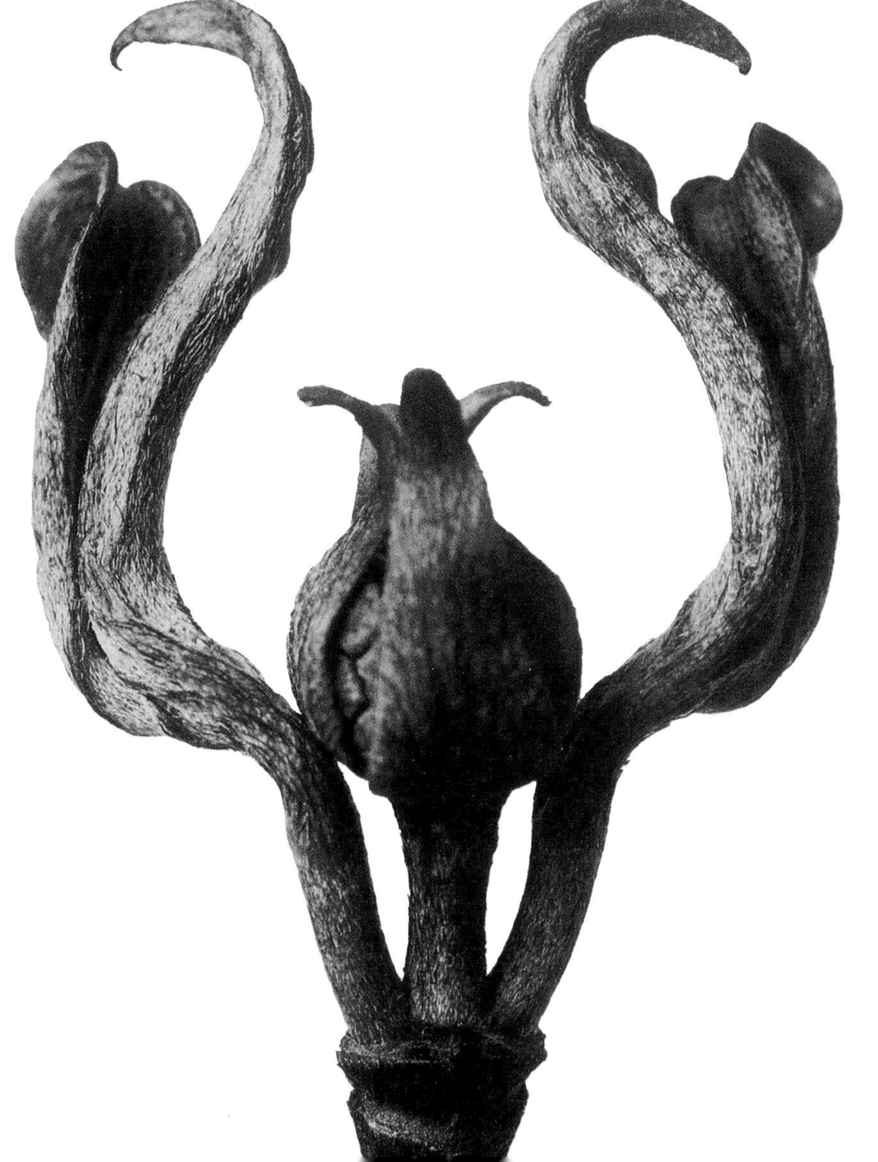

KARL BLOSSFELDT: MODELLER • PHOTOGRAPHER • COLLECTOR OF PLANTS

He photographed plants by the thousands – photographs which feature flowers, buds, branched stems, clusters or seed capsules shot directly from the side, seldom from an overhead view, and rarely from a diagonal perspective. He usually placed the subjects of his photographs against white or grey cardboard, sometimes against a black background. Hardly ever can details of the rooms be detected. The light for his shots was obtained from northern windows, making it diffuse, yet the light came from the side, creating volume. The technique and processing conditions were very simple; only the size of the negative format was more demanding. Nothing should detract from the subject. This man produced such pictures for over thirty years and producing them was nothing but work.

This line of work was not his main profession, although his fame today rests on his photographs. Rather, plant photography was part of an all-inclusive whole, a teaching concept, for which he was only partly responsible. He taught for over thirty years at the Kunstgewerbeschule in the Charlottenburg quarter of Berlin. Shortly before his death, he announced his intention to publish his teaching methods. Neither this plan nor that of completing an archive of plant photographs was ever realized. What has remained are bundles of photographs, which have made history on their own, and the memory of a teacher, who – like so many in his field – left no lasting impression outside of his personal sphere.

The man's name was Karl Blossfeldt, and his life's achievement occupies a firm place in the history of 20th-century art, although the aims of his undertaking place him

firmly within the 19th century. Blossfeldt shares this bridging of two centuries with other great collectors in the history of photography such as the Parisian Eugène Atget, and it is to this bridging of two centuries that his influence may be attributed today. In contrast, the course of Karl Blossfeldt's own life has little significance for his own pictures.

Born in the Harz Mountains in central Germany, Karl Blossfeldt grew up in the country surrounded by plants and animals, which he enjoyed drawing and modelling. His education included an arts and crafts apprenticeship, a craftsman's scholarship for further education in drawing and some musical instruction, about which sparse secondary biographical sources provide no details. He appears to have wavered between a career as a relief sculptor and that of a singer's rehearser, until he was given the task which was to determine his life's work. He was asked to produce models for drawing classes in accordance with Moritz Meurer's method. Meurer, Blossfeldt's teacher at the Kunstgewerbeschule, had been commissioned by the Prussian Handelsministerium (which managed the Kunstgewerbemuseum and the school as a way of promoting the state economy) to improve the drawing instruction for craftsmen and manufacturers. In this regard he suggested in a memorandum that portfolios and collections of models of plant samples be created for use as motifs for ornamental design. On the one hand, the students were to learn from the samples; on the other hand, the manufacturers were to gear their pattern designs to them. In 1890 Meurer settled in Rome, and was assigned six assistants who had all won scholarships to work with him. They were to work on drawings or cast models for him. The four artists in Meurer's train included Otto Dannenberg and Max Seliger, later to be academy directors. One of the two casters was Blossfeldt.

Moritz Meurer and his assistants not only collected, drew and cast botanical specimens in Rome and its outlying regions, but also systematically photographed plants. Rather than taking shots outside in nature, they employed the method traditionally used for slide preparation, thereby al-

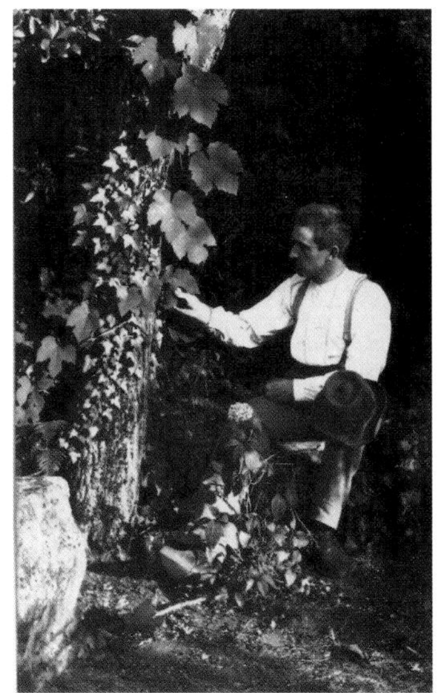

Karl Blossfeldt in Italy, c. 1894

tering the very substance of the plant. Shoots were removed from stems, roots cut back and, if necessary, buds opened. The products prepared in this way, the plant types, were stuck on a support, mounted before a uniform background, and exposed. In the history of photography the adoption of this method, with its roots in painting, was a tradition in itself. The inventors of this photo technique (Talbot and Bayard, Steinheil and Kobell) used a paper negative to take positive copies – the forerunner of the photogram – and proved the scientific usefulness of their work into the deal. Around 1850, the Austrian mathematics teacher Constantin Freiherr von Ettinghausen developed the system for his teaching method from plant photographs. Photographic publishing houses, such as that of the Strasburg photographer Adolphe Braun, stocked and sold rolls of plant photographs. At the same time as Meurer and his assistants were in Rome, a class for photomechanical printing processes was established at the Leipzig Academy, whose director, Georg Aarland, had successfully published botanical books.

The question of how Meurer and his assistants, in particular Blossfeldt, actually photographed plants can only be inferred indirectly from the first publication of the project, dedicated to a single plant – acanthus (cow-parsnip) – and its influence on ancient art. Two of the photos bear Blossfeldt's name. They show the leaf and stem of the acanthus with the characteristic pointed tips and crenature on the head, pictured before a grey background. In 1896, when the book about the acanthus was published, Moritz Meurer returned to Berlin, albeit continuing in subsequent publications to cite his address in Rome. Scholarships and commissions were temporarily suspended. What followed was an enormous number of books, newspaper articles, correspondence courses and lectures, which advanced Meurer to probably the most influential applied-arts educator of the German Empire. All publications included many reproduced drawings, a few reproduced reliefs and castings, and some photographs by either Meurer or Blossfeldt; the majority were attributed to Blossfeldt.

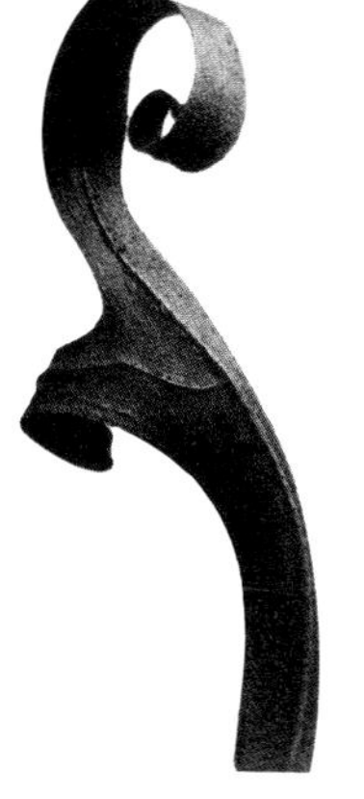

Much has been surmised about the cooperation between Meurer and his assistants, particularly with regard to Blossfeldt's photographs. The original plan – to prefabricate decorative basic-cast forms as rough workpieces for industrial use which only needed to be technically adapted and appropriated – quickly proved itself to be impracticable. For this reason Blossfeldt, trained as a caster, had to specialize in collecting plants, or face the loss of his scholarship and therefore his work. In contrast, Meurer was an experienced plant photographer, already familiar with the extensive literature on sources and portfolios for artists, which included a diversity of botanical books. As a young man Blossfeldt had already been an amateur photographer and was therefore quite willing to be trained in the field.

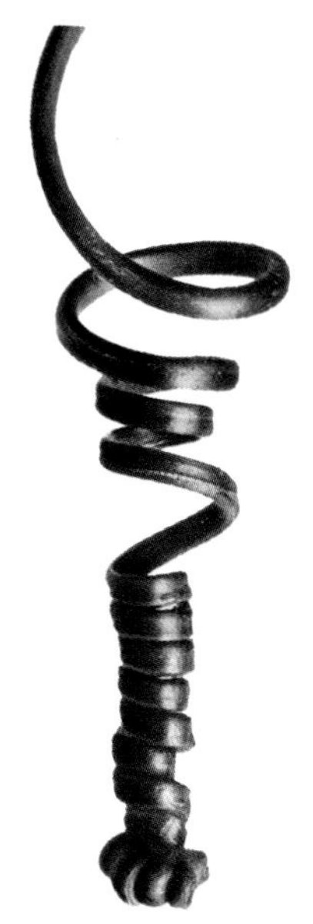

Although the beginnings of Blossfeldt's work on plants began in Rome, this part of his œuvre should not be overestimated in relation to the whole. The same holds true for Meurer's influence on Blossfeldt's type of instruction and the picture forms which grew out of it. For a time Blossfeldt went through a phase of reorientation, undecided whether to stay in Italy, emigrate to the United States, or assume employment in the German arts and crafts industry. In the end, he chose a position as an assistant teacher and assistant director for modelling from plants at the Kunstgewerbeschule in Charlottenburg. In 1899 he was elevated to the post of lecturer. This enabled him to combine all his areas of interest – the study of nature, meticulous drawing, and the sculptural transposition of drawings into relief. At a time when this university in Berlin was setting out to become the leading institute of instruction for budding industrial designers, the students not only learned graphic arts and furniture design but also devised modern modes of transportation, urban architecture and industrial products. In no way was the drawing and casting of plants superfluous embellishment. Blossfeldt's task in his beginners' classes was essentially that of demonstrating that the best constructions for industrial designs had already been anticipated in nature.

This view of the structural detail as the pattern for possible

industrial design, with particular regard to the prudent application of the means, is linked specifically to the thinking of Gottfried Semper and the 19th century with its belief in progress. However, it goes beyond that in several aspects. Blossfeldt cited climatic and technical reasons for using photographs as drawing copies. Quite simply, plants decayed too quickly to be used for intensive study. At the same time, taking photographs, and the requisite systematic approach, enabled Blossfeldt to make the object secondary and to incorporate into his class preparation the structural principles which were to be taught. Unlike anyone before him, he made technical and creative aids work for him.

Blossfeldt photographed plants in front of a grey or white background. In doing so, he was drawing inspiration from the pharmaceutical plant catalogues and classification books of the late Middle Ages and the herbariums of the 17th and 18th centuries, in which comparison and classification of the plants shown had only been possible by employing a uniform background. However, Blossfeldt dispensed completely with the practice of his contemporaries in the media who loathed empty backgrounds: no room should be empty, no wall devoid of decoration, no newspaper, magazine or book page should be printed without filling every last inch with ornamentation and trimming. Yet publishing his photos as part of the arts and crafts movement of the time was a notion which did not occur to Blossfeldt. For him, they represented nothing more than teaching material.

The plant photographs were produced by simple means. Legend has it that a relatively straightforward home-made camera was used, one common in its time and not very large, with a format of 9 x 12 cm. The glass plates which served as negatives were coated with inexpensive but not completely neutrally coloured orthochromatic emulsion. They were occasionally coated with panchromatic emulsions, making possible a neutral reproduction of the colour red into a mid-grey value. It was only after 1902 that such emulsions became widely available. Since the emulsion was thin and therefore enabled high contrast with extremely sharp edges,

it served especially to stress the structural elements. It was thus used primarily for photographs with white or grey backgrounds. The rarer photos with panchromatic emulsions were used to illustrate entire clusters or beds of flowers with a wider variation of colour or grey values.

The most significant advance in Blossfeldt's photo technique was in the processing stages. Rather than making prints from developed negatives or using the gum process or carbon prints (both popular at the time), Blossfeldt made slides for projection. The most common slide format before World War I (8.5 x 10.5 cm) corresponded more or less to Blossfeldt's format; he could then select the desired section of the photo by blocking out the rest with black strips. There are no records of the projection of his slides as drawing copies. We know of two methods of projection employed around 1919, however, of which he surely also made use. One method was to project the slides onto the wall and have the students draw from the enlarged projection. The other method, used in textile design, involved reflecting the projected photo with mirrors onto the drawing board, where the students simply traced over the contours. This last exercise reduced drawing to a mere formality with little relation to plants. On the other hand, in terms of repeated patterns and mechanics, it offered more possibilities for the application of the drawing. For such a projection to serve the mechanical copying of formal properties, the slides had to fill one precondition: they had to show the object clearly and without extraneous details. This was exactly the quality of Blossfeldt's work, and in particular the quality of his collection of plant photographs.

Karl Nierendorf must have recognized the stark modernity of this approach to photography when he was first confronted with Blossfeldt's plant photos in 1925. Nierendorf, a banker versed in Dada, Precisionism and Constructivism, had become a gallerist and impresario, moving from Cologne to Berlin. The wealth of legends surrounding the avant-garde has succeeded in throwing a veil over this first meeting. But it is more than obvious that the time was right

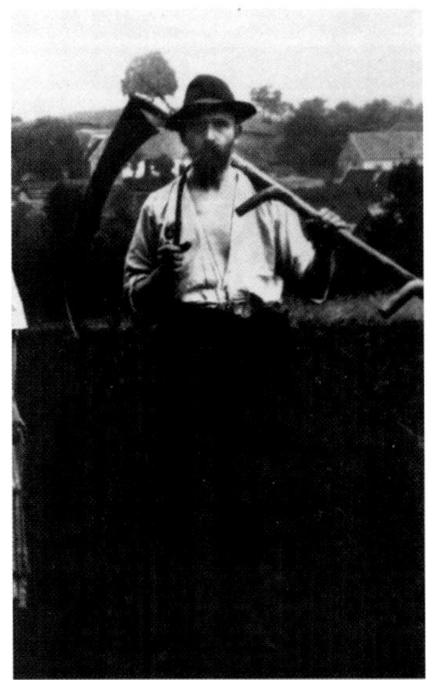

Karl Blossfeldt in the Harz Mountains, c. 1920

for the publication of these photos. In 1925 the term "Neue Sachlichkeit" (New Functionalism) was coined at an exhibition; the first books on the new type of plant photography were published, works by Ernst Fuhrmann, Martin Gerlach, Albert Renger-Patzsch and Paul Wolff; and simple object photos predominated in textbooks such as László Moholy-Nagy's "Painting, Photography, and Film". The avant-garde artists, in many ways stimulated by the developments in the fledgling Soviet state, dreamed of an art which would change society, assisted by a new idea of technology based on construction. Feats of engineering became the preferred objects for art criticism and Blossfeldt's photographs made for splendid comparison. Werner Lindner demonstrated similarities between the architectural structure of a tower and Blossfeldt's photo of field horsetail. In the journal "UHU", there was even talk of "green architecture".

All of these publications appeared without a single exhibition of Blossfeldt's photographs, but probably on the strength of the slides he had used for teaching. Not until 1926, and particularly after 1928, were these plant photographs exhibited. That was the year in which the epochal "Urformen der Kunst" ("Art Forms in Nature") was edited by Nierendorf on Blossfeldt's behalf at the renowned architectural publishing house of Ernst Wasmuth. In this way, the photos began to lose the status of teaching material which they had occupied for thirty years. László Moholy-Nagy awarded them a prominent place in his planning for the "Film und Foto" exhibition of avant-garde art in Stuttgart in 1929. In the space of one year, "Urformen der Kunst" went into a second edition and was translated into several foreign languages.

After 1930 there was scarcely a major photo exhibition, and certainly no important annuals, in which Blossfeldt was not represented. In the autumn of 1930, Karl Blossfeldt had reached retirement age and gave up teaching in order to devote himself to the evaluation of his plant archives. His second book of photographs, "Wundergarten der Natur" ("Nature's Wonderful Garden"), was published in the spring of 1932. The paucity of solo exhibitions of these photographs

indicates, however, that the book was the actual medium of his work. In the preface to "Wundergarten", the only text from Blossfeldt's pen, he not only hinted at the forthcoming publication of his drawing instruction, but also conveyed an idea of the fundamentals of his work. A rough, extremely conservative mélange, his philosophy was part romantic view of nature, part critique of functionalistic design, and part reductive application of Darwinism to both social and aesthetic developments. This fit the political climate of the time shortly before 1933, yet it also showed that Blossfeldt had not understood his own influence on the avant-garde. On December 3, 1932, Karl Blossfeldt died in Berlin.

Blossfeldt's work has never been forgotten. New editions of "Urformen der Kunst" and foreign language versions of "Wundergarten" are continually being published, photos from both books have been used in compilations of every sort, and there have been references to their educational context. In the 1950s, the fourth and fifth editions of "Urformen der Kunst" were instructional pillars at German design schools and an essential part of their basic-studies programmes. Not until the middle of the 70s, however, when photography was finally accepted as an art form in itself, did Blossfeldt's plant photos achieve international recognition. Thus began the analysis of plant photography according to aesthetic principles. The details of plant stems and seed capsules in front of a pure white background very quickly became the motifs by which the entire work was identified.

This has had somewhat disagreeable posthumous consequences for Karl Blossfeldt's fame. In the same manner in which the industrial photos of Hilla and Bernd Becher were seized upon, Blossfeldt's work process has been declared a principle of style and either criticized or copied. Scarcely a single object has been photographed without a white background, and the subjects for photo series have escalated. Such illustrations could also refer to plants, thereby revealing two interpretations of Blossfeldt's achievement. Yasuhiro Ishimoto, Robert Mapplethorpe and Christopher Williams, to name representatives of one camp, have intensified

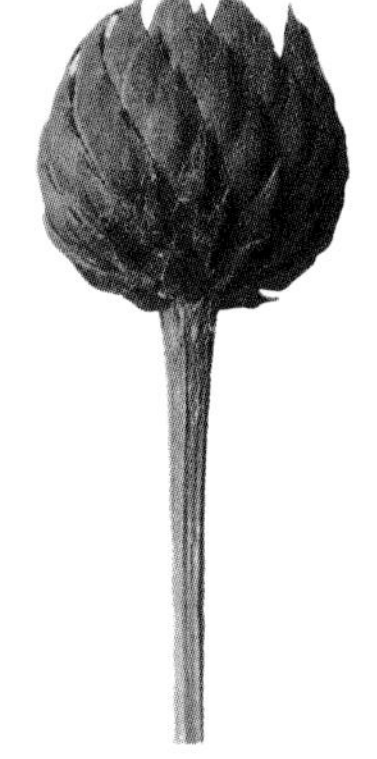

the beautifying aspect of these photos and perfected the technique of duplication, the brilliance of the lighting and the quality of the blow-up. In contrast to Blossfeldt's photographs, which usually did not exceed a medium-sized format, those of the above-mentioned artists often occupy entire walls. The other camp criticizes the notion of prettified display and, staging objects of horror before the camera, shoots the pictures in Blossfeldt's straightforward style, rendering them instances of horrifying recognition. Among such photo series, which often include macabre, cynical texts, are Joan Fontcubertas' herbarium, Reinhard Matz's packaged sausages, and Shomei Tomatsu's catalogue of radiated objects from Nagasaki.

A collection of motifs which adopts Blossfeldt's means of staging is always concerned with a general ambivalence of photographic interpretation. This ambivalence is historically determined by the repeated debate over Albert Renger-Patzsch's first collection of photographs and its title "Die Welt ist schön" ("The World is Beautiful"). Even the most distinct photos of objects cannot guarantee that that which is presented exists as it is presented, or that the object will be perceived by the viewer in the same way as the original implied. Blossfeldt's plant collection problematized this notion on several accounts. If the formal aspects of his herbarium are highlighted at the expense of exact biological classification, then the structural elements can no longer always be interpreted as positive signs of human civilization. However, it seems probable that viewers are motivated to look at these photos through an awareness that many of the plants (and with them their structural value) are irrevocably lost, forgotten or relegated to the past. All the new photo series since Blossfeldt have made this an issue. Whether through ironic distance or formal perfection, they all demonstrate the dubious success of a way of thinking which has forced the view of nature into its own mechanistic perspective.

It is therefore not surprising that versions of Blossfeldt's plant collections are now available as computer programmes (simulation is used where what is available is insufficient).

The result is a recourse to post-mediaeval herbariums. The simulated plant growth such programmes demonstrate is no different from the cut-outs of the world which Renaissance artists showed in their encyclopaedias. They too supplemented the known with the imagined, changing the common to the beautified. No plant can grow so perfectly as it does on a computer screen, yet no computer-simulated plant is natural. For Blossfeldt, replacing nature with a mechanical likeness was a small, efficient step in his teaching method. By making daily excursions into the countryside around Berlin and Rome, he was able to reverse the abstract. What is decisive for his contemporary followers is the consciousness that all plant catalogues are inevitably connected with the disappearance of what is catalogued. The pleasure on viewing these photographs sharpens the realization that even if the object viewed has not disappeared, its continued existence is in danger.

Rolf Sachsse

The young shoot behaves from the beginning with all the dignity of a tree, – but to create a basis for its future life, it sends out its branches to form a strong, straight trunk, to hold it firmly above the ground.

(John Ruskin, 1860)

Equisetum hyemale
Rough horsetail
Shoot tip magnified 25 times

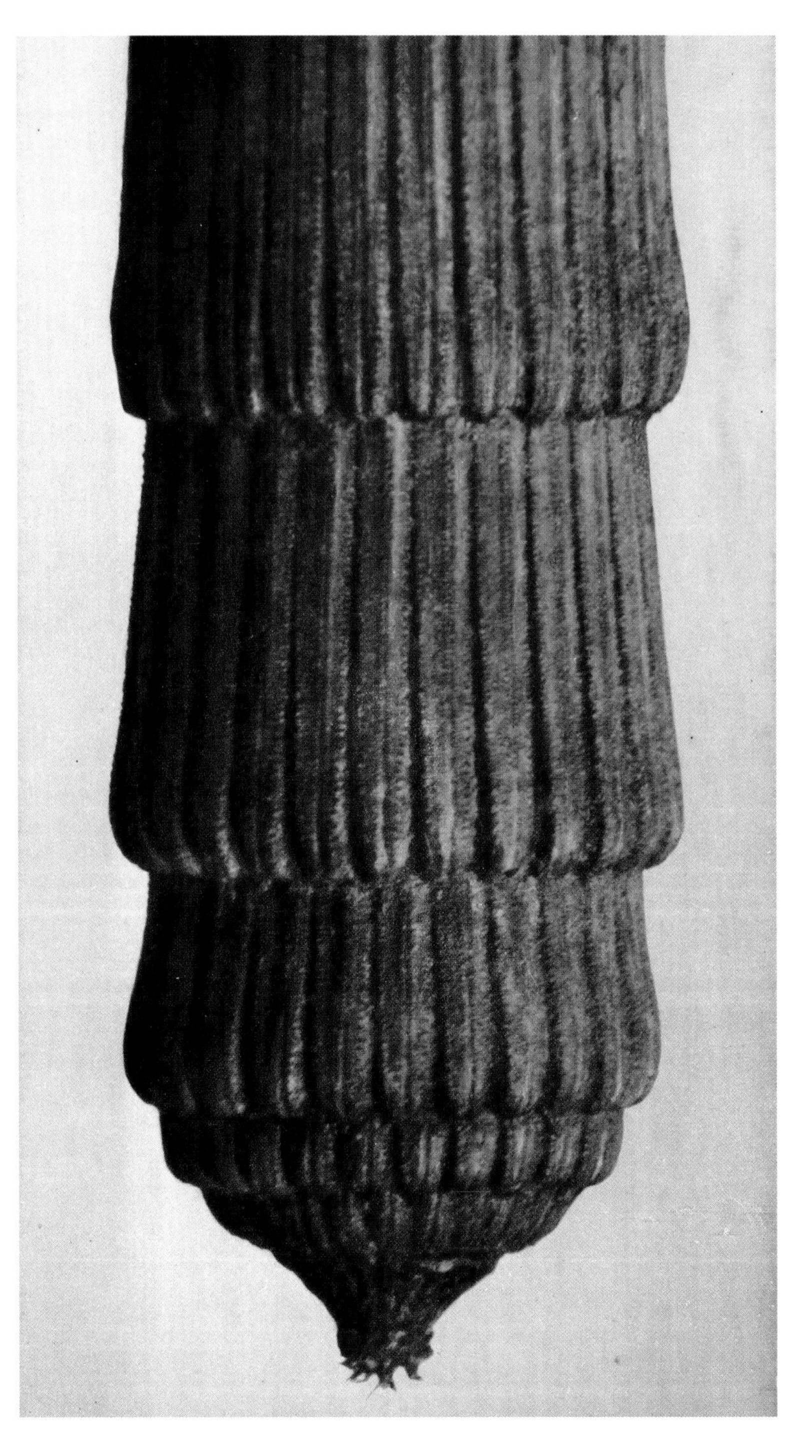

Geometry is in everything, one finds it everywhere, it is nature's greatest teacher. One must be familiar with it, if one wants to observe and understand the things of creation.
(Eugène Emmanuel Viollet-le-Duc, 1879)

Equisetum hyemale
Rough horsetail
Cross-section of a stalk magnified 30 times

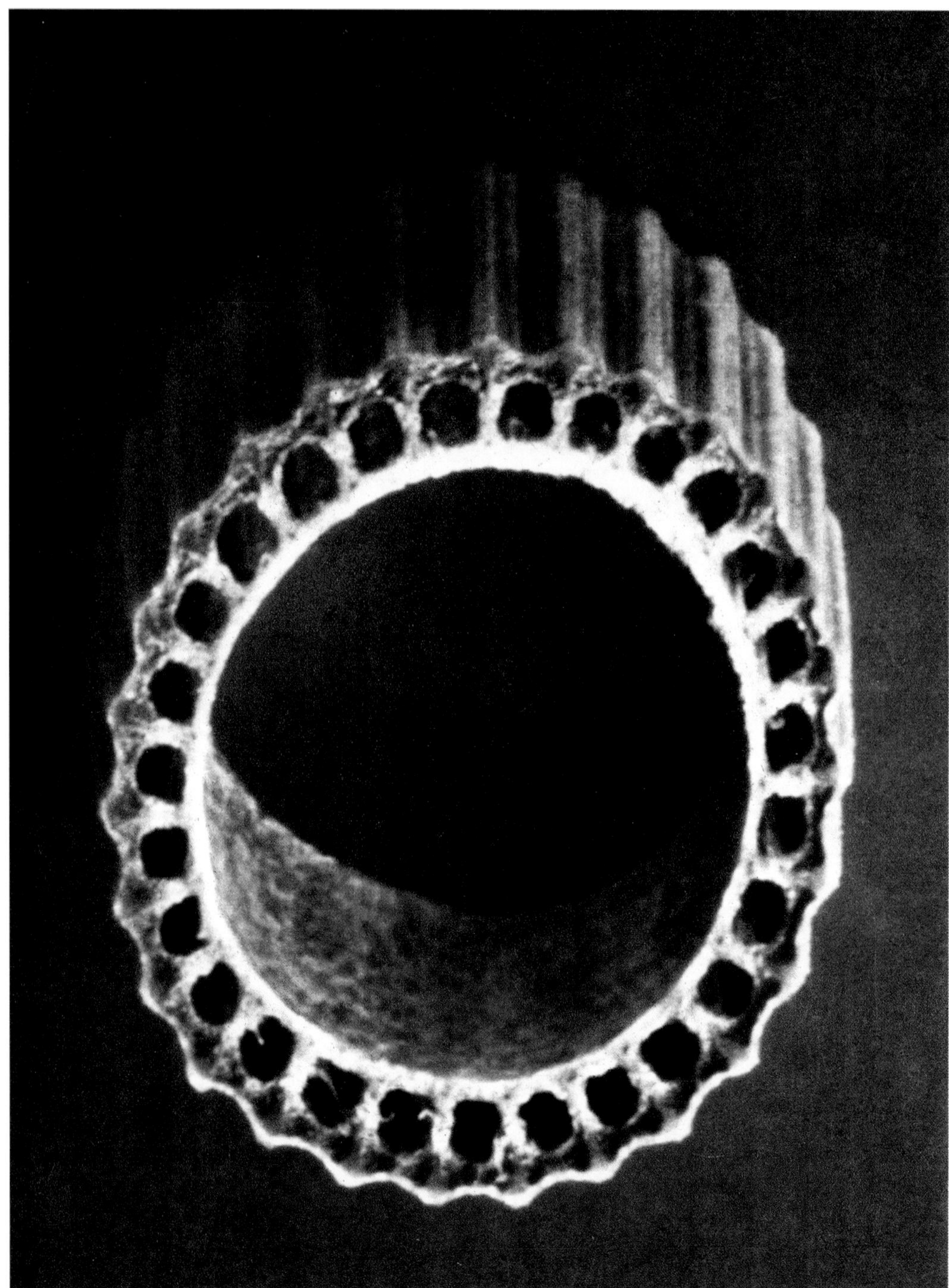

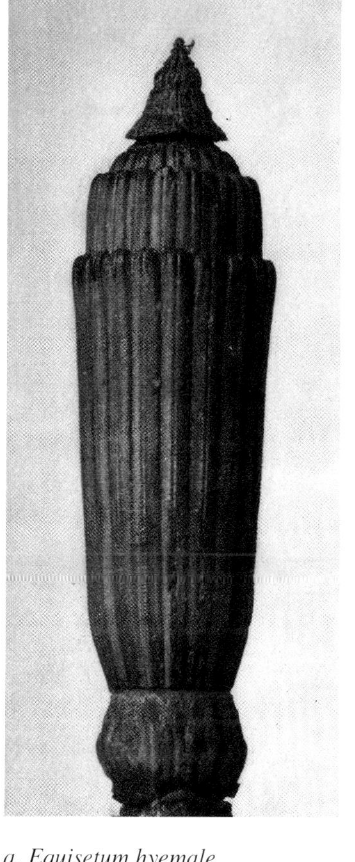

a. Equisetum hyemale
Rough horsetail
Magnified 12 times

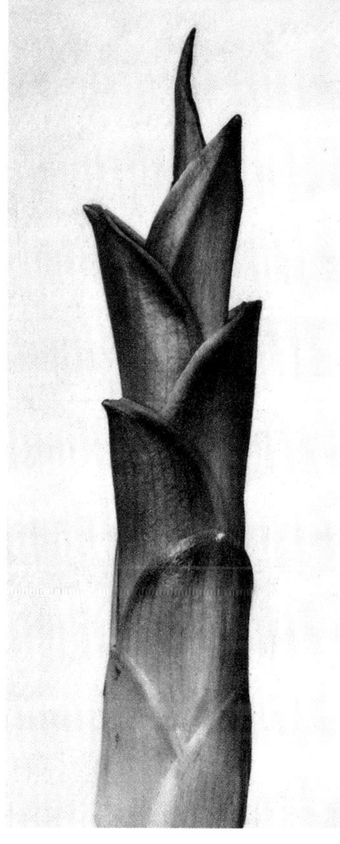

b. Hosta subcordata
Young shoot
Magnified 4 times

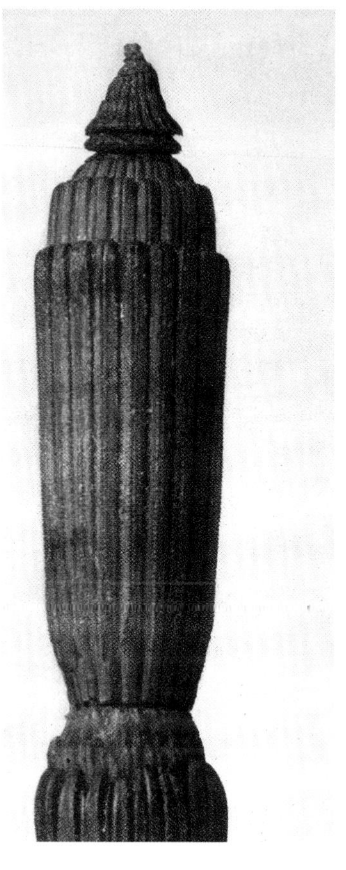

c. Equisetum hyemale
Rough horsetail
Magnified 12 times

Equisetum hyemale
Rough horsetail
Stalk parts magnified 8 times

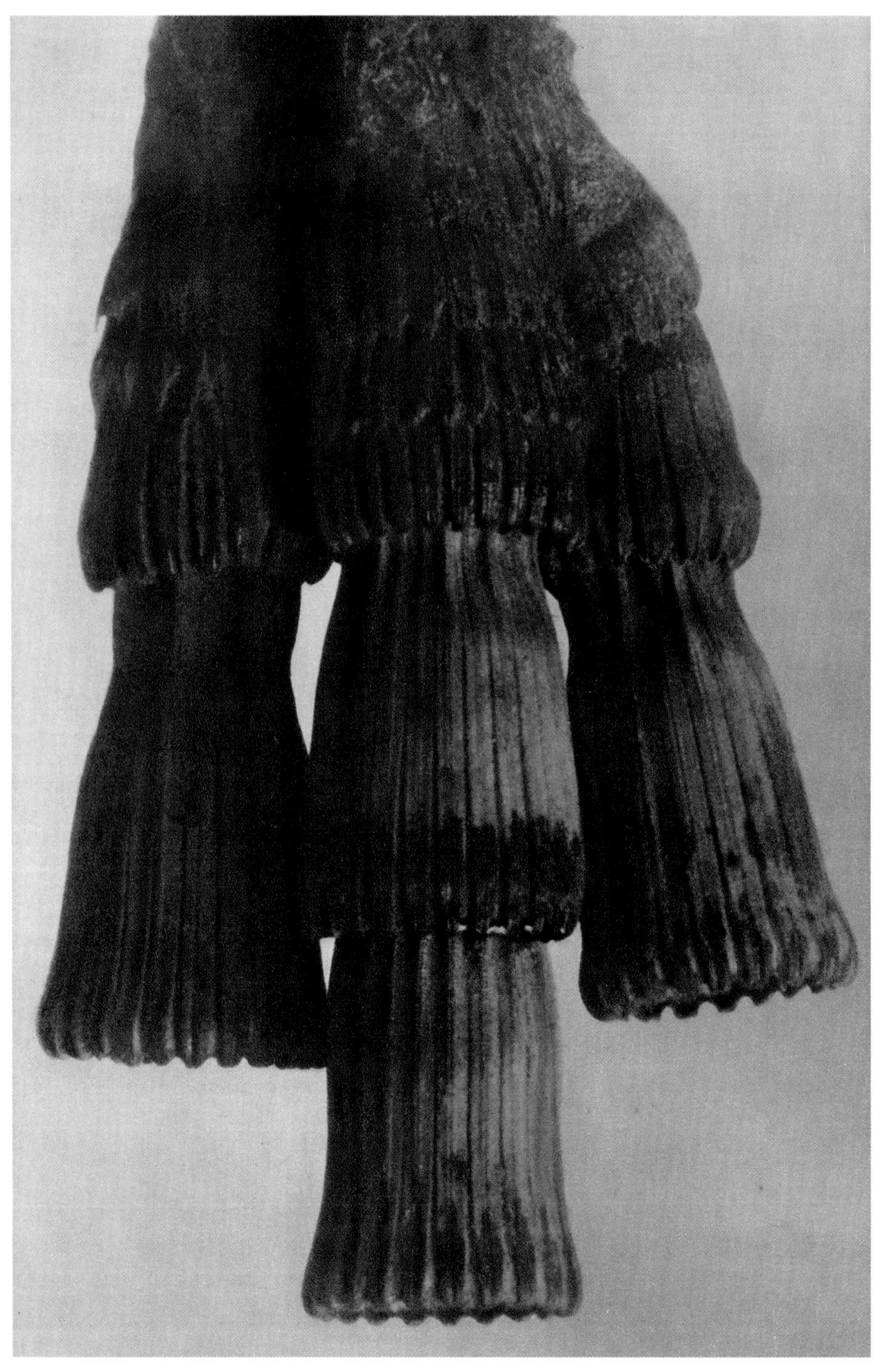

Since only simple forms lend themselves to graphic representation, I cannot make use of lush flowers such as a gardener raises and am dependent almost exclusively on wild plants. To this end, I now make bicycle trips and short excursions by train into the countryside around Berlin. If, for example, I find an interesting plant today near Potsdam, tomorrow near Friedrichshagen and the day after tomorrow at Teufelssee or in Dalldorf, then I am forced to make a country outing each day to the place in question for a period of three or four months in order to search for this one plant. I do not mind doing this, even if it means sacrificing my mornings and sometimes even my days off.

(Karl Blossfeldt to Bruno Paul, 1901)

Aesculus parviflora
Horse chestnut
Branch tips magnified 12 times

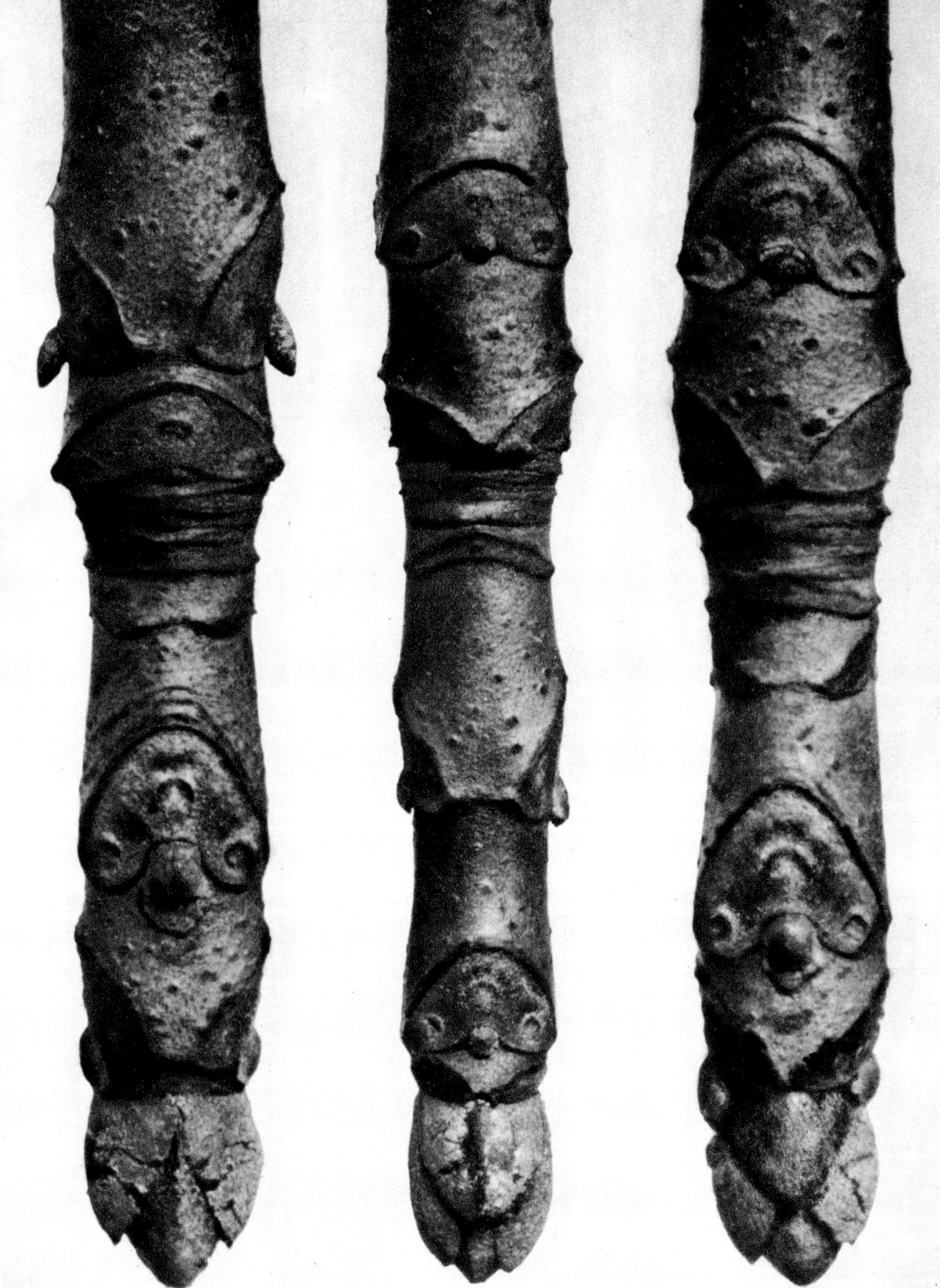

In everyday use the word 'ornament' signifies all the artistic adornment of our technical works. In particular, we make a distinction by referring with the word 'ornament' more to the outward decoration of a product, while we call its inherent features the 'art form.'

(Moritz Meurer, 1909)

Impatiens glandulifera

Indian balsam

Stem with branches, life-sized

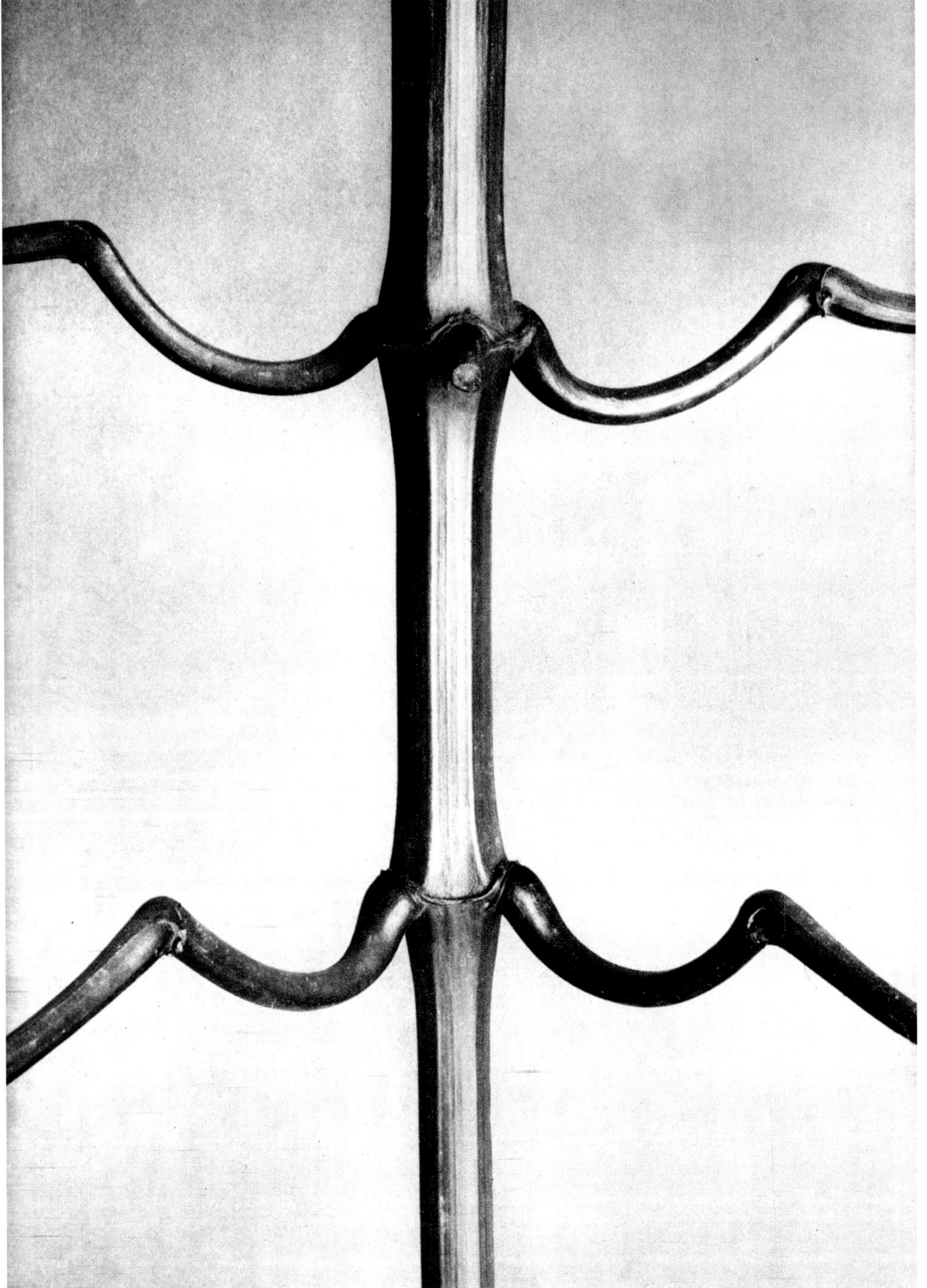

PHOTOGRAPHS ON THE FOLLOWING PAGES:

a. Saxifraga paniculata
Saxifrage
Leaf rosette magnified 8 times

b. Saxifraga willkommiana
Willkomm's saxifrage
Leaf rosette magnified 8 times

c. Aconitum anthora
Monkshood
Magnified 3 times

d. Eryngium bourgatii
Sea holly
Magnified 5 times

e. Saxifraga willkommiana
Willkomm's saxifrage
Magnified 18 times

Acer rufinerve
Maple
Branch with leaf buds magnified 10 times

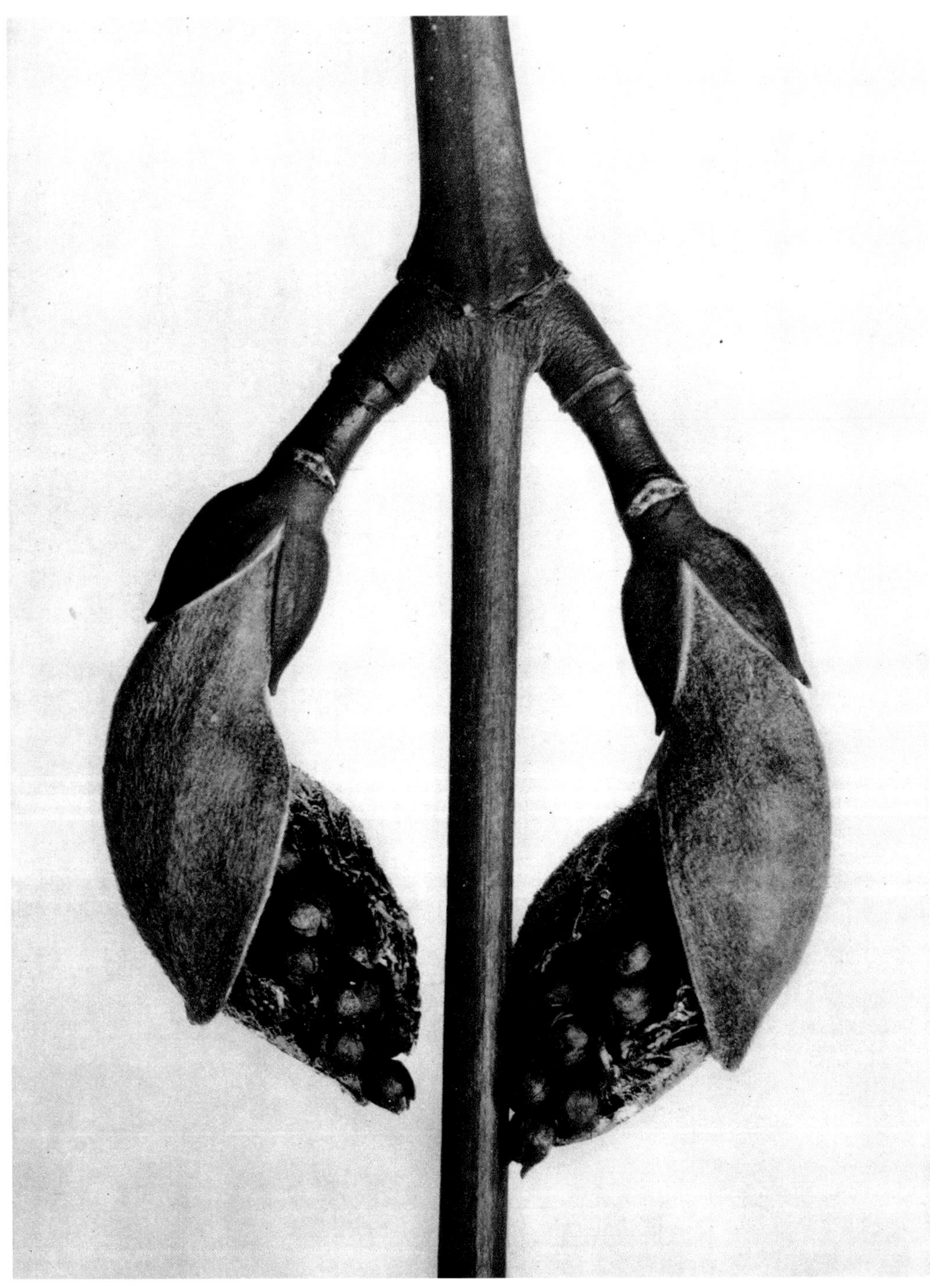

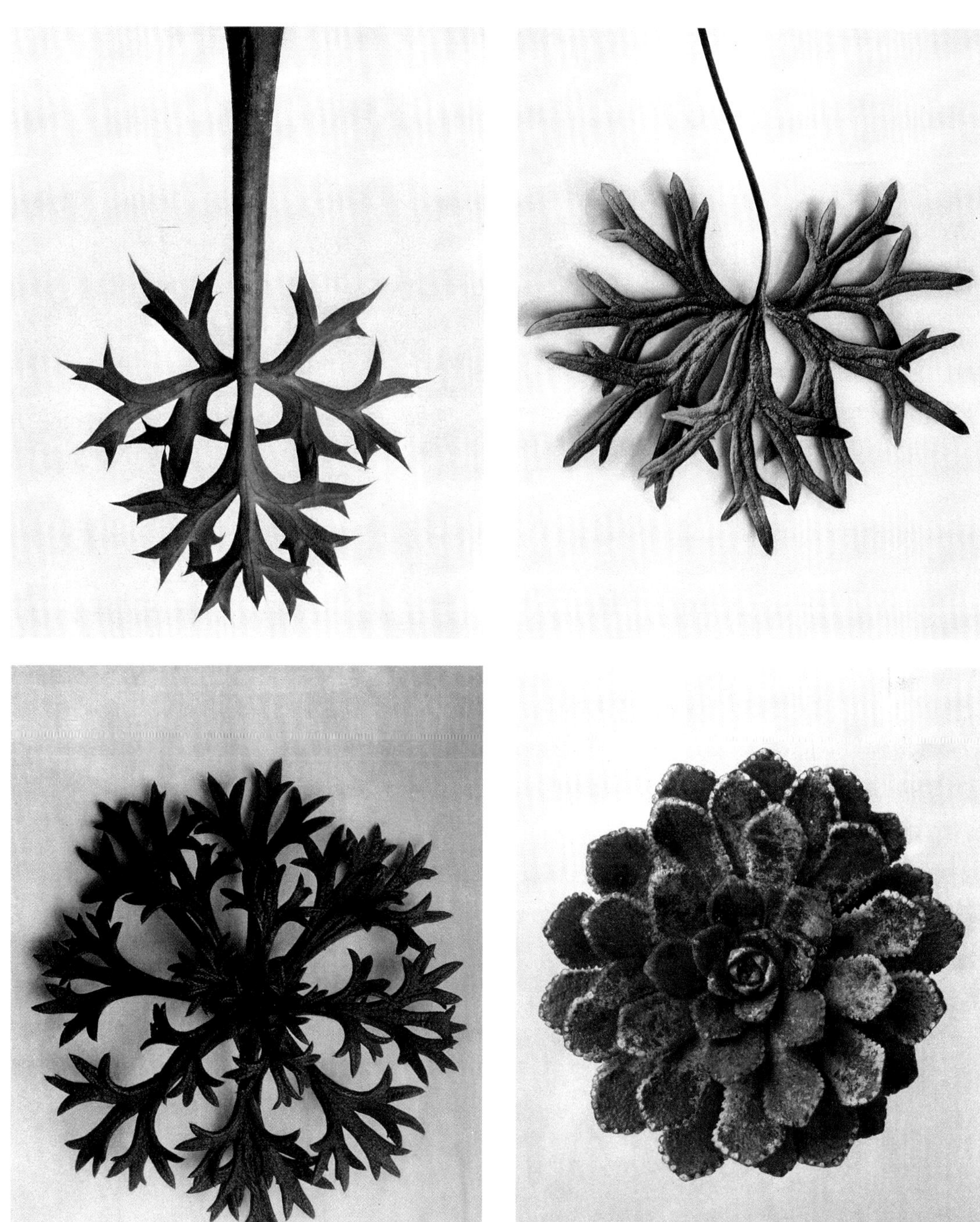

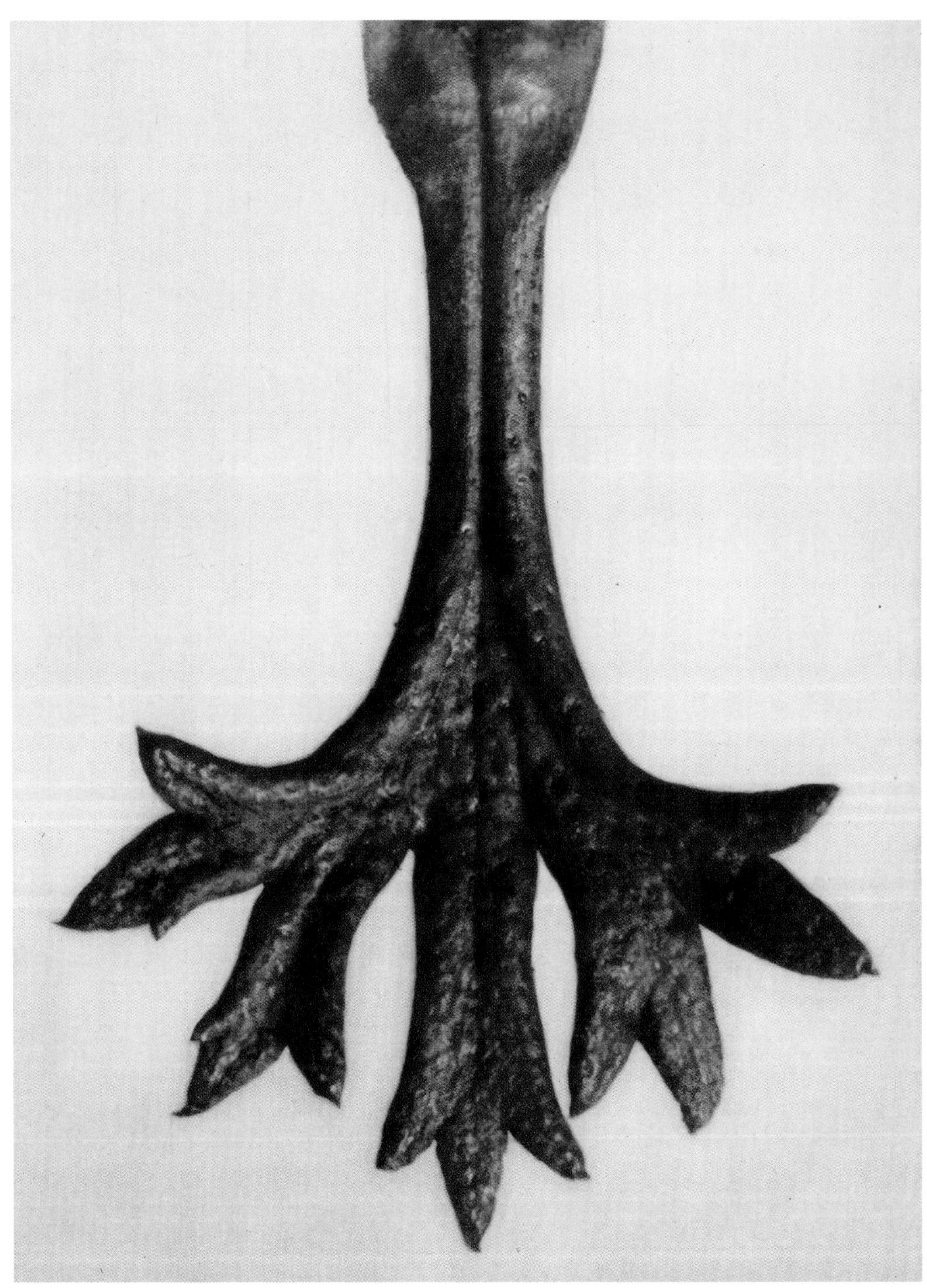

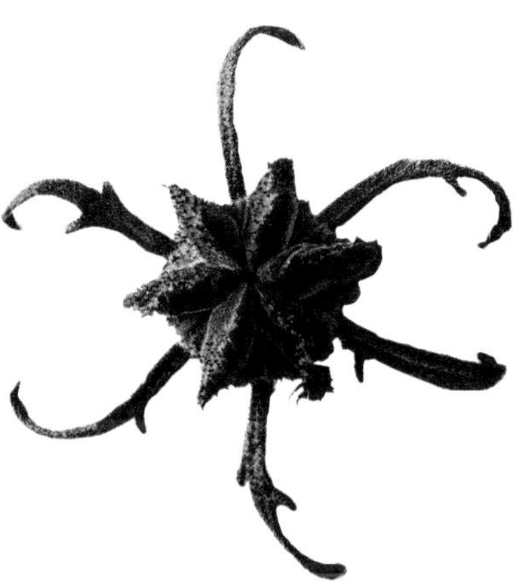

Cajophora lateritia, Loasaceae
Loasa
Seed capsules magnified 5 times

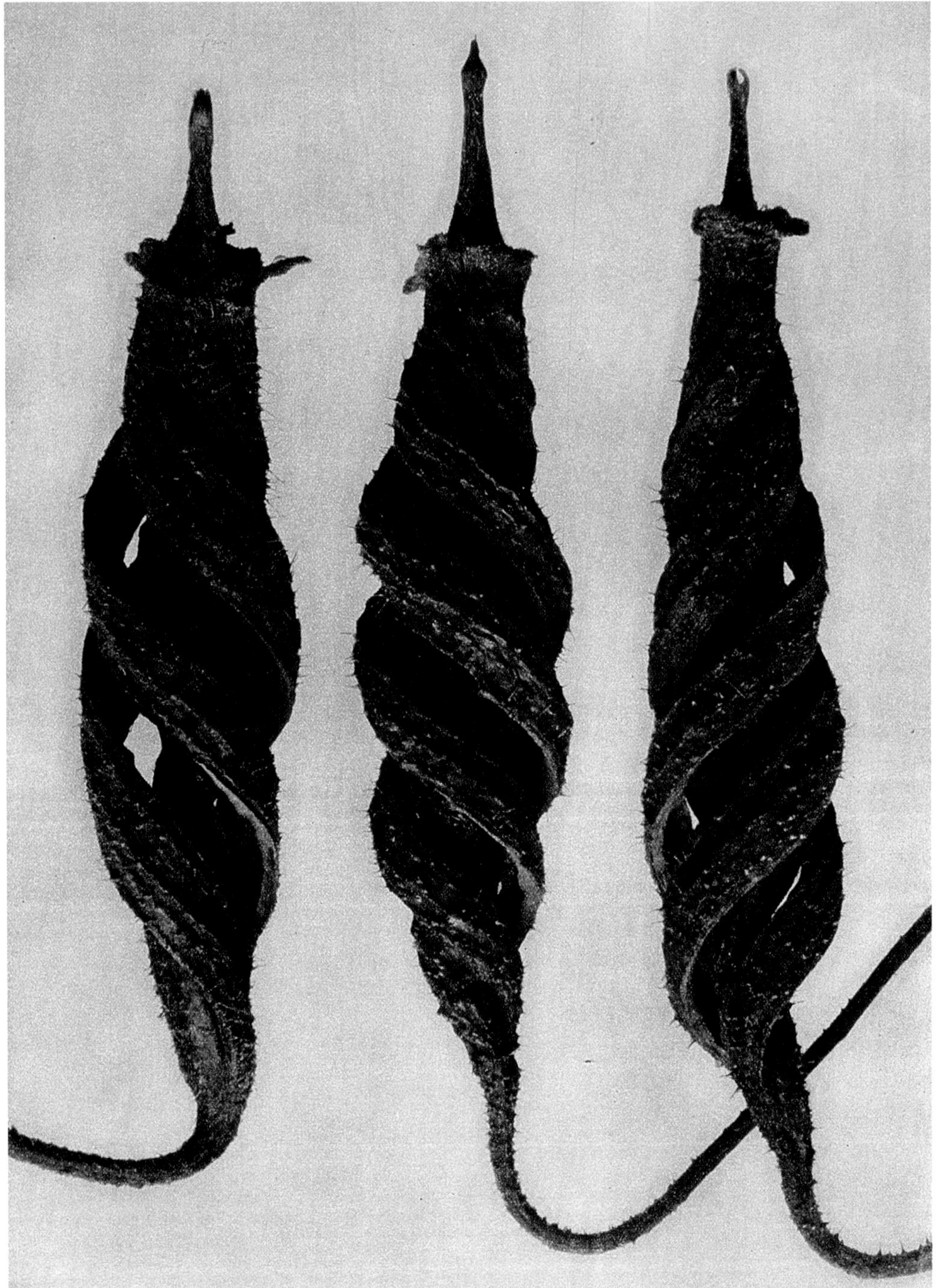

Those who have never been moved to raptures by the tender curve of a blade of grass, the wonderful sternness of the thistle, the rough youth of sprouting leaf-buds; and those who have never been touched to the depths of their soul by the massive appearance of a tree root, the imperturbable strength of riven bark, the slender pliancy of the birch, the enormous tranquillity of a canopy of leaves – know nothing of the beauty of form.

(August Endell, 1909)

Phyllitis scolopendrium
Hart's tongue
Young curled fronds magnified 6 times

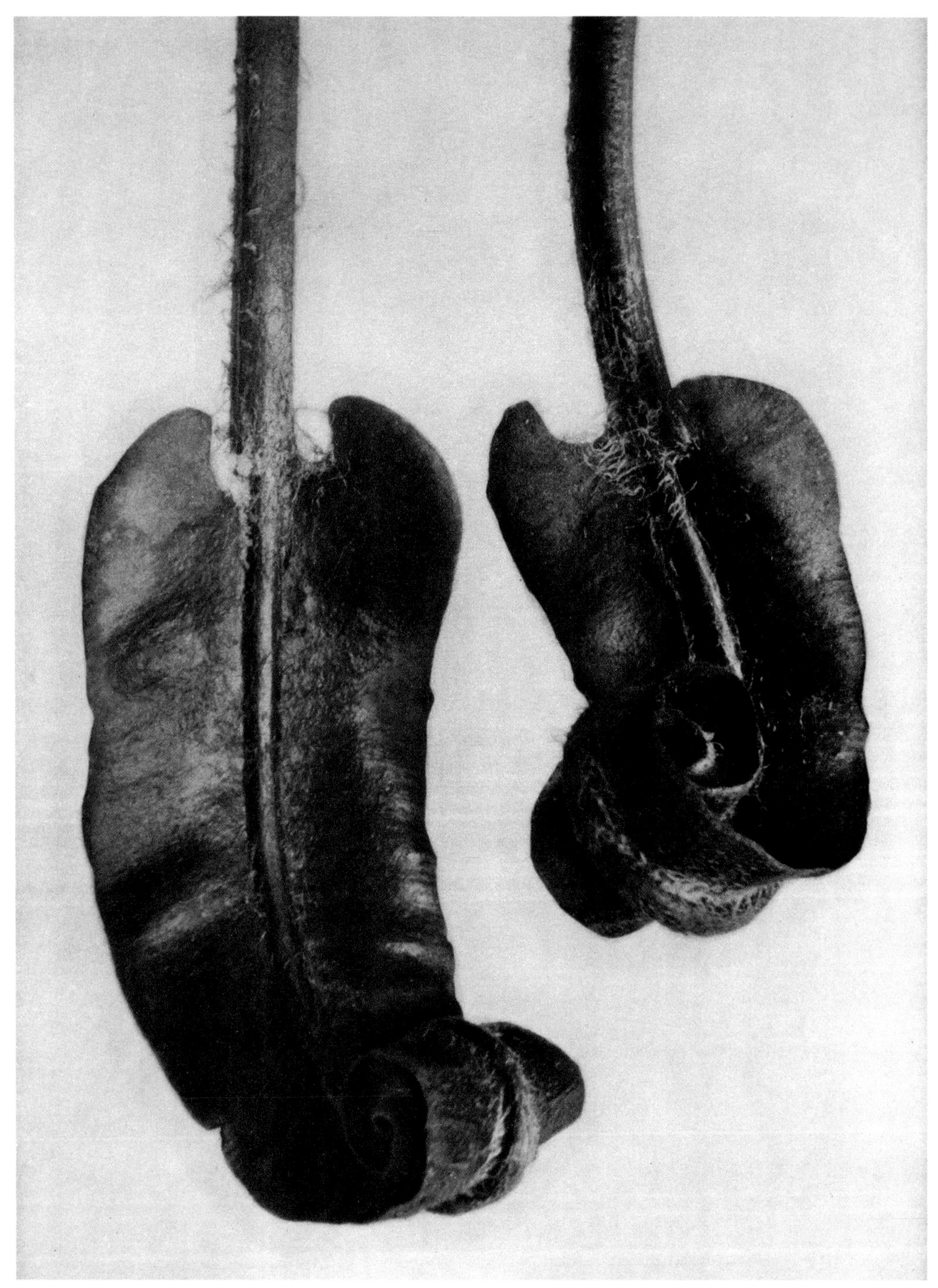

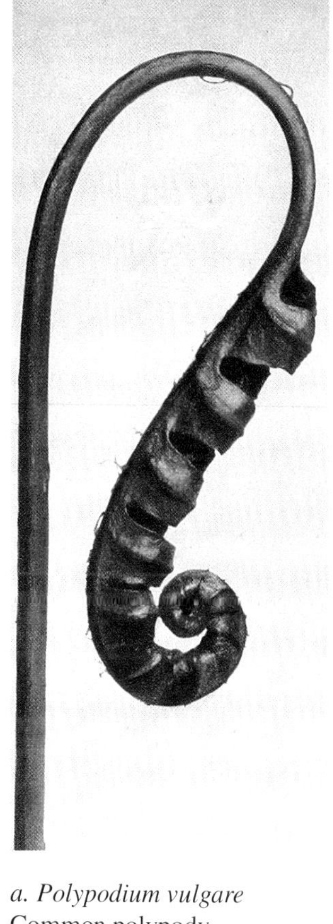

a. Polypodium vulgare
Common polypody
Young frond magnified
7 times

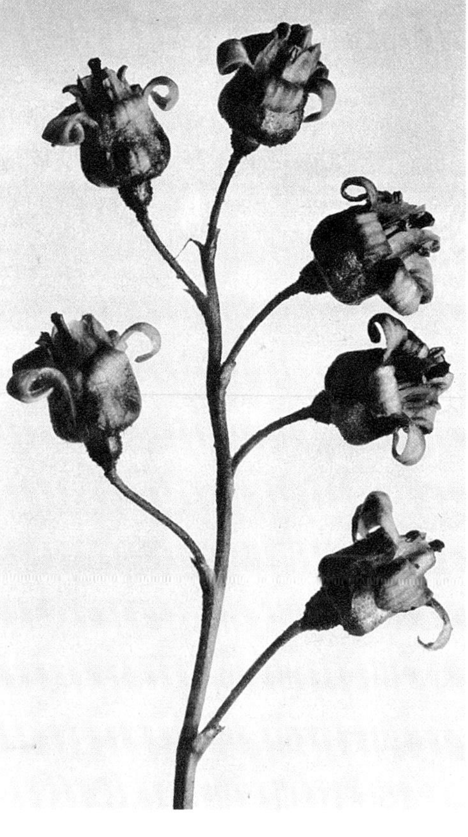

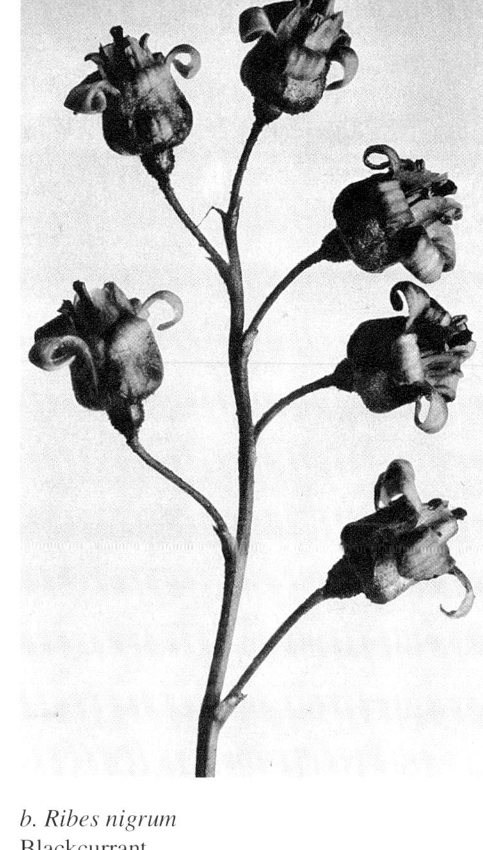

b. Ribes nigrum
Blackcurrant
Cluster of flowers magnified
5 times

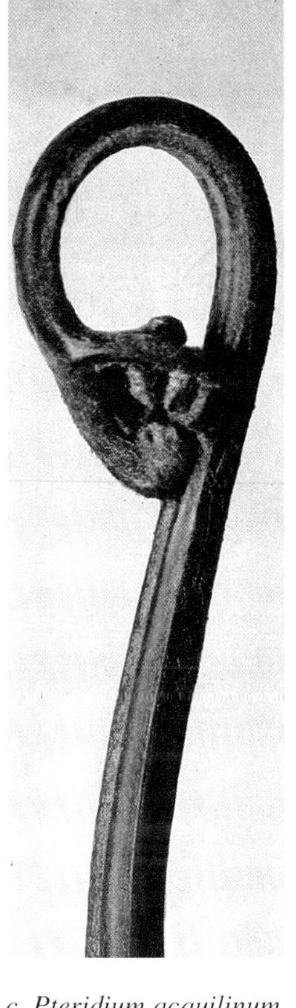

c. Pteridium acquilinum
Bracken fern
Young frond magnified
5 times

Polystichum munitum
Shield fern
Young curled leaf magnified 6 times

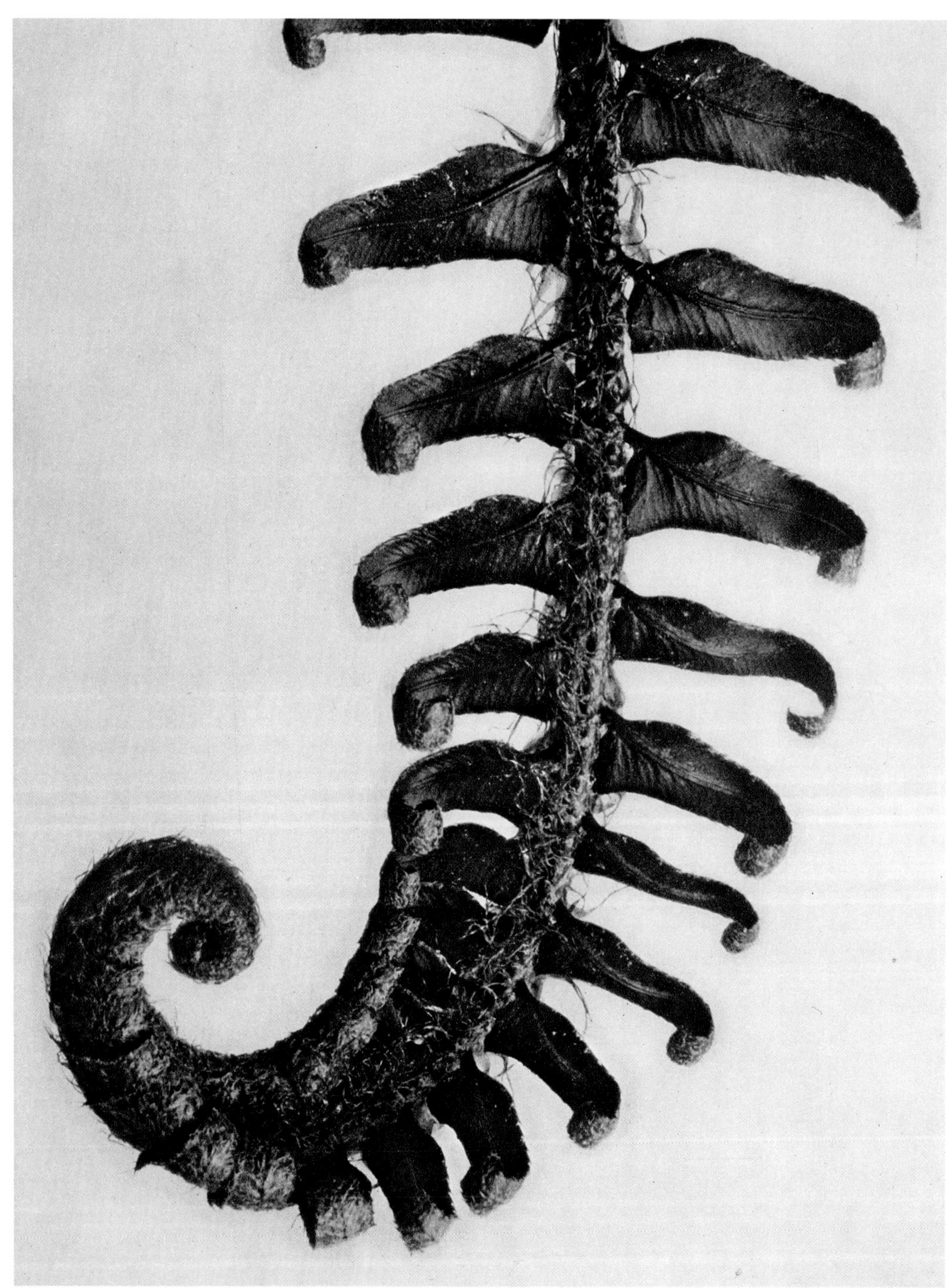

Art and nature, the two great phenomena of our environment, are so closely related that the one is inconceivable without the other, and it will never be possible to force them into a formulaic definition.
(Karl Nierendorf, 1928)

Delphinium
Larkspur
Part of a dried leaf magnified 6 times

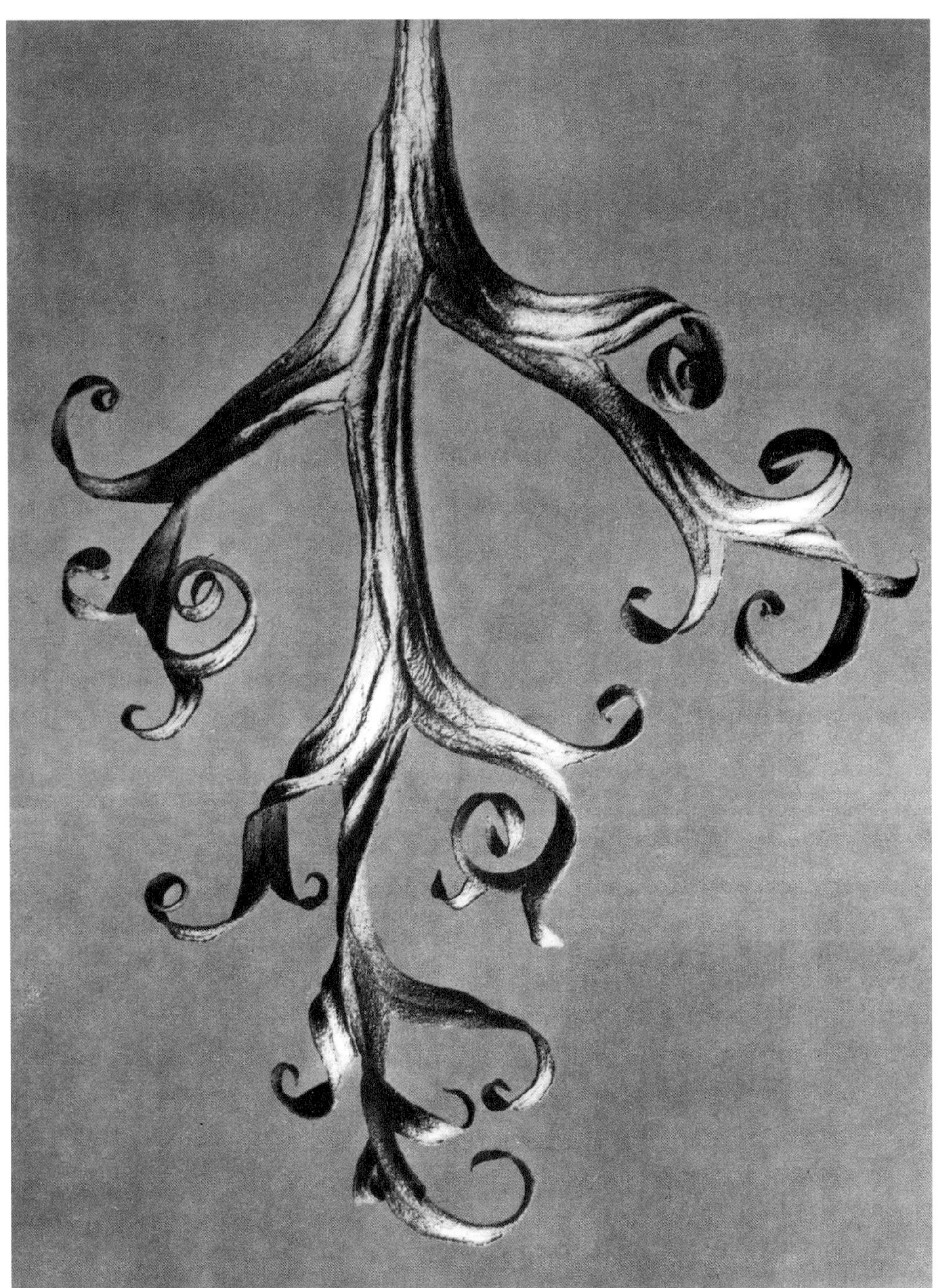

PHOTOGRAPHS ON THE FOLLOWING PAGES:

Matteucia struthiopteris
Ostrich-fern
Young curled frond magnified 8 times

Dryopteris filix mas
Common male fern
Young curled fronds magnified 4 times

Dipsacus laciniatus
Teasel
Leaves dried on the stem magnified 4 times

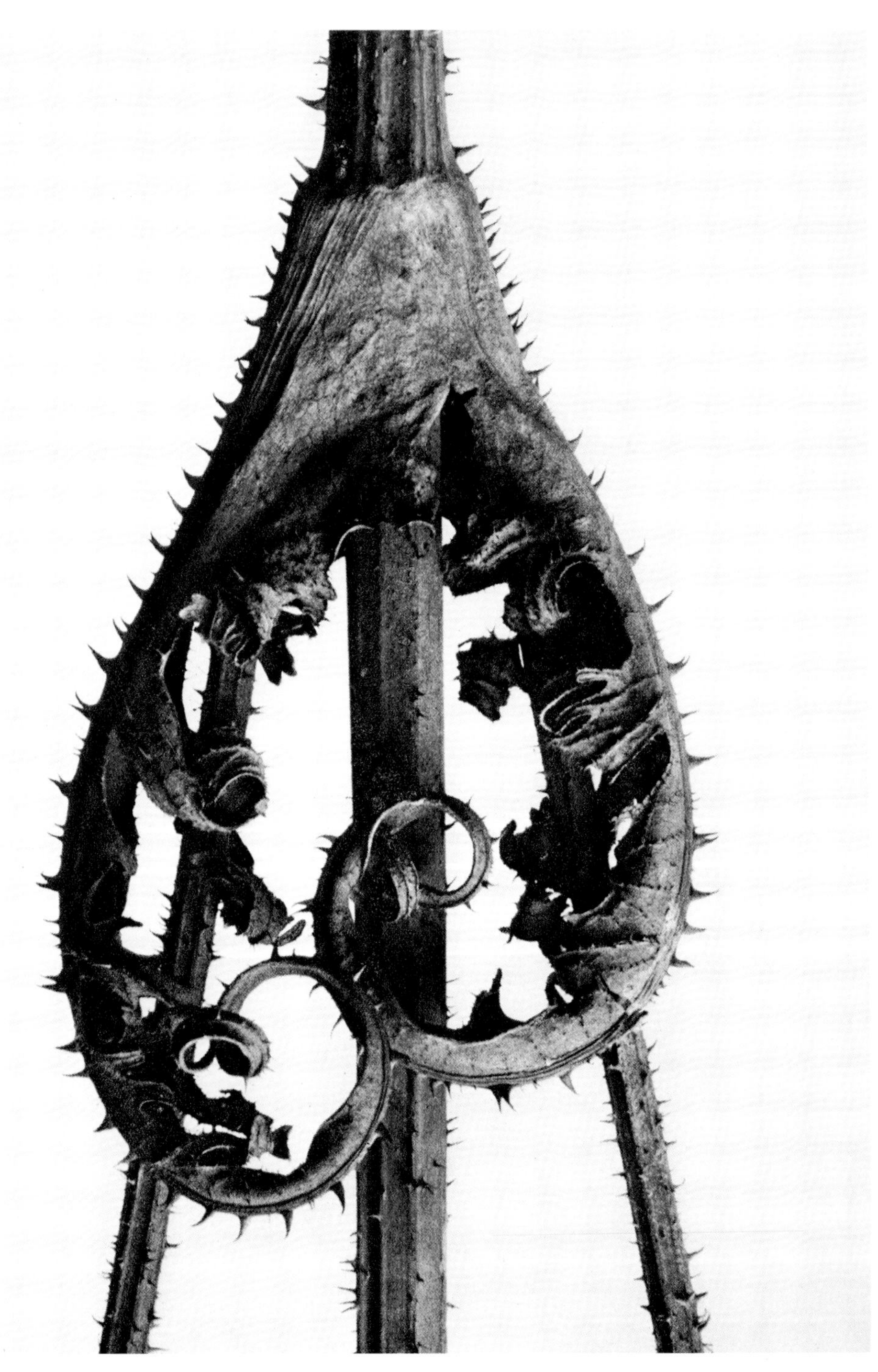

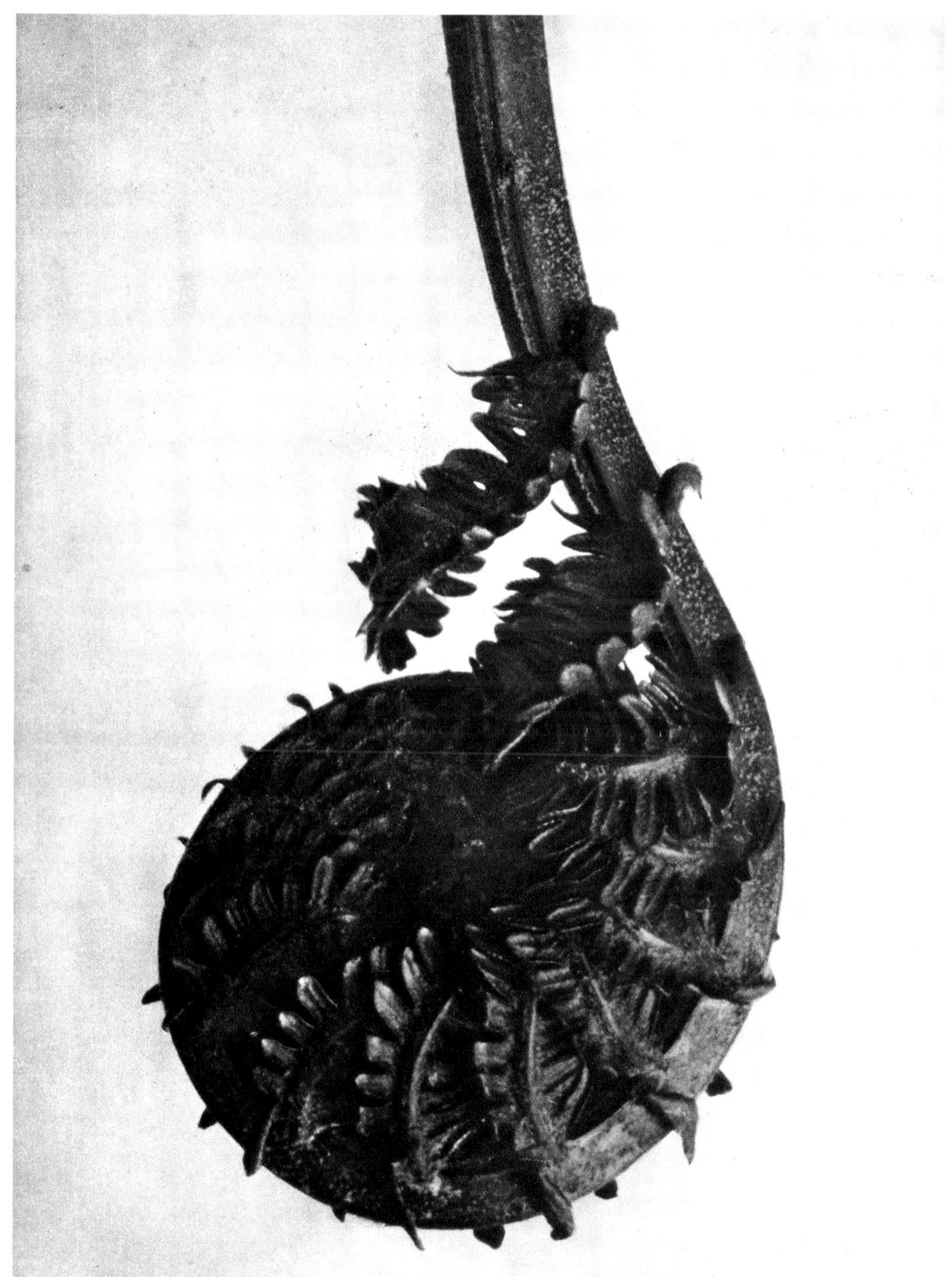

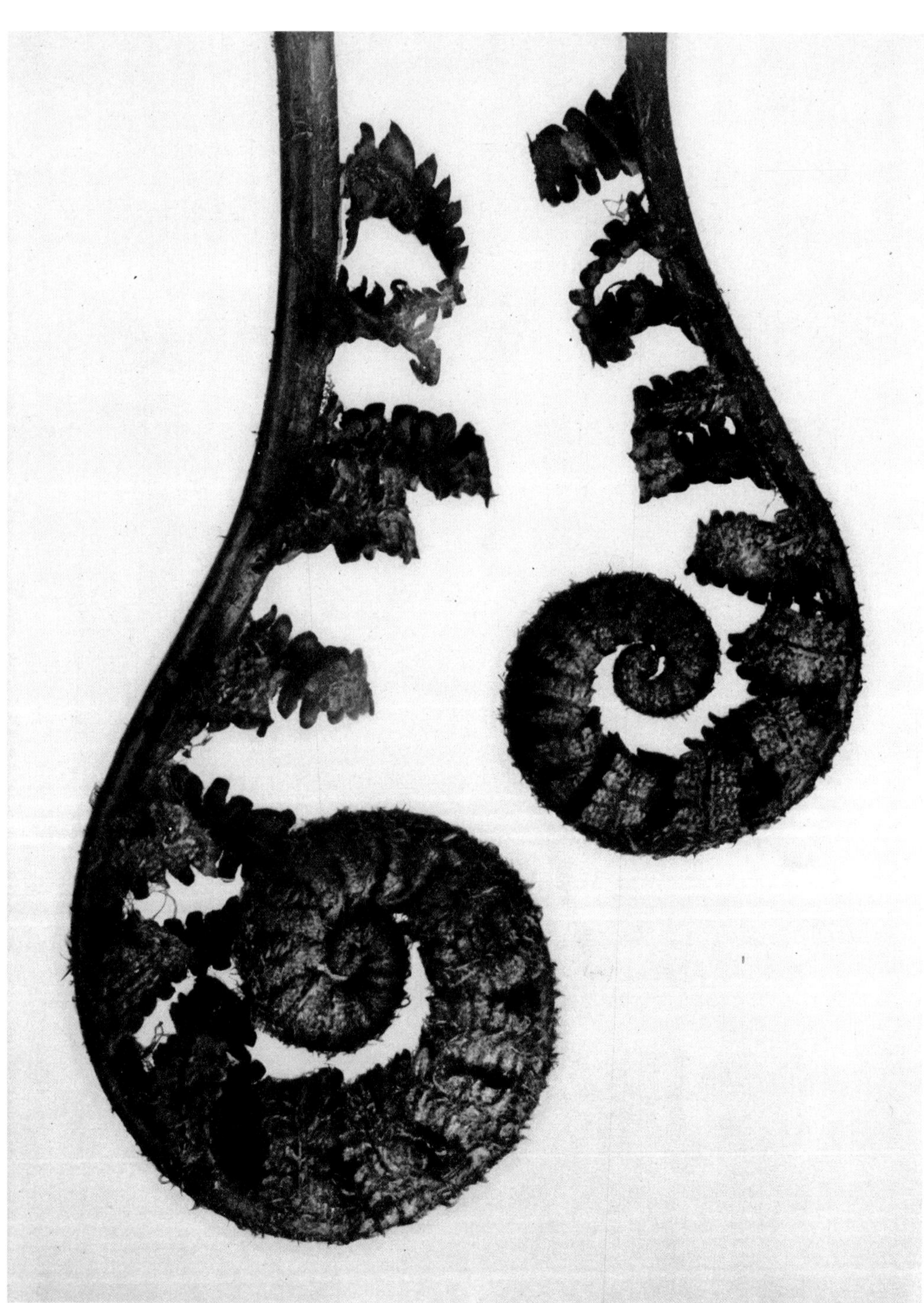

These photographs reveal a completely unexpected wealth of analogies and forms in the plant world. Only photography is able to do this, since it requires powerful enlargement before the forms lift the veil which our laziness has thrown over them…
(Walter Benjamin, 1929)

Bryonia alba
White bryony
Leaf with tendril magnified 4 times

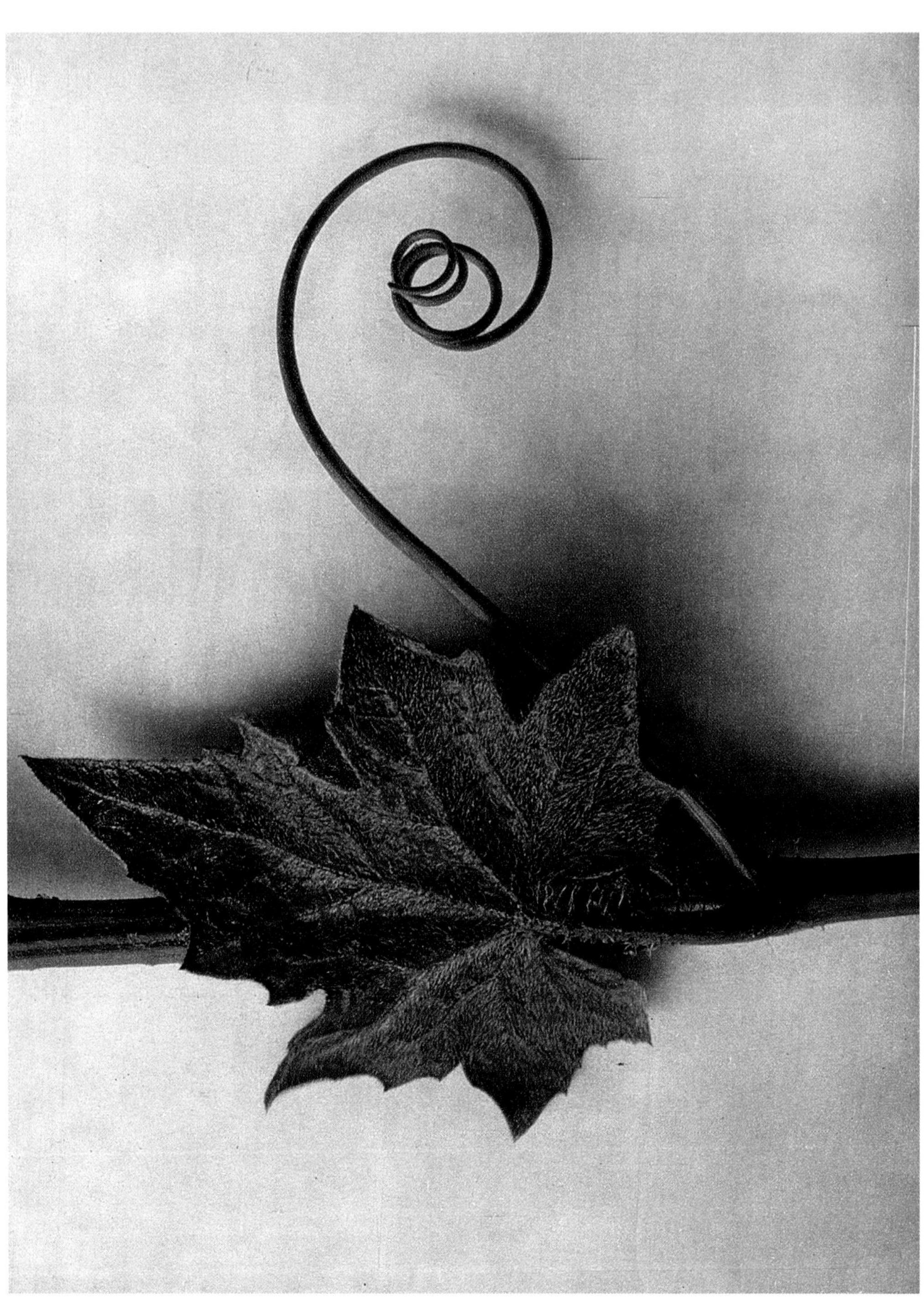

But the plant never falls into the sober representation of a mere object; it forms and grows according to logic and function, and, with primeval power, forces everything to the most sublime artistic form.

(Karl Blossfeldt, 1932)

Cucurbita
Tendrils of a pumpkin
Magnified 4 times

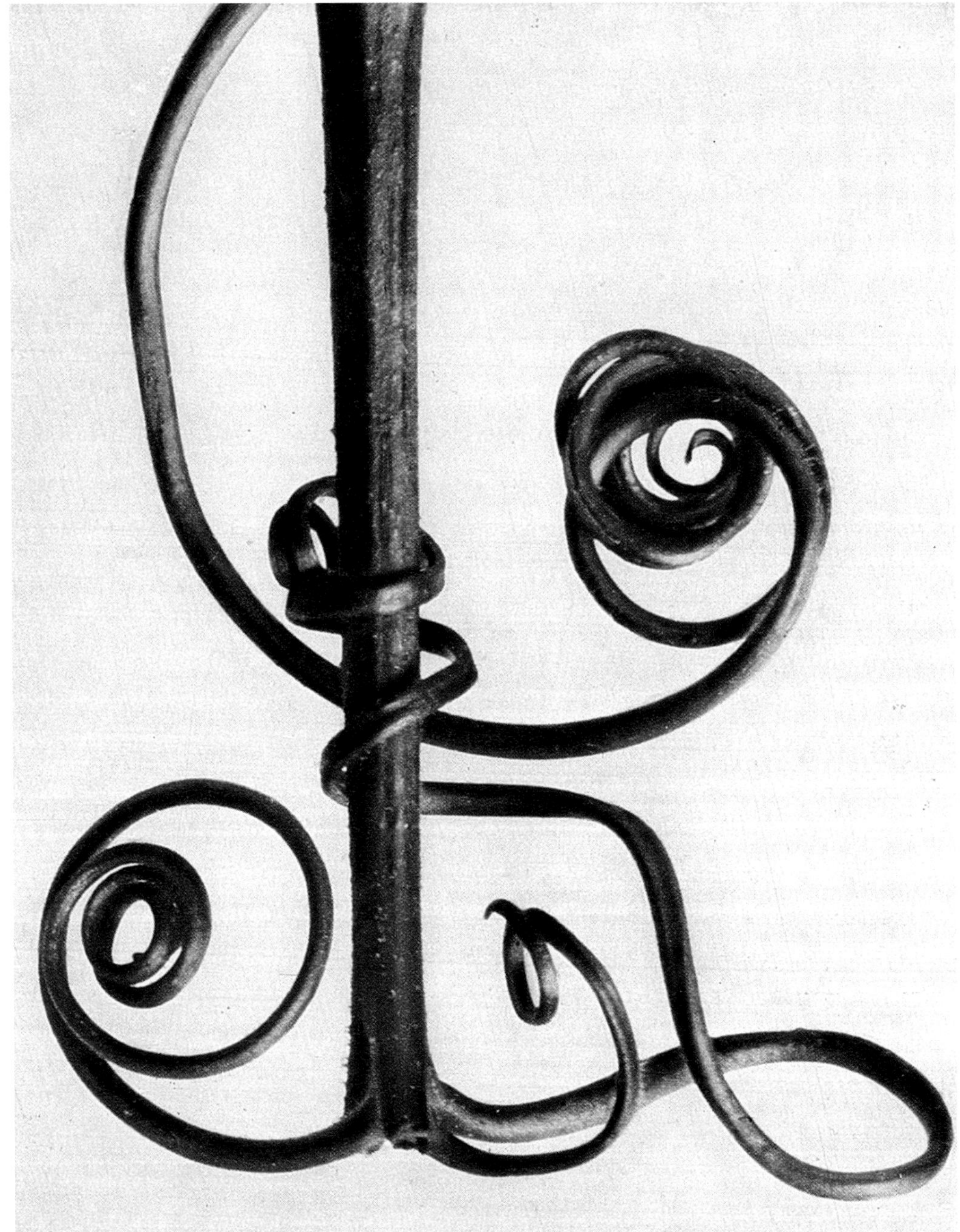

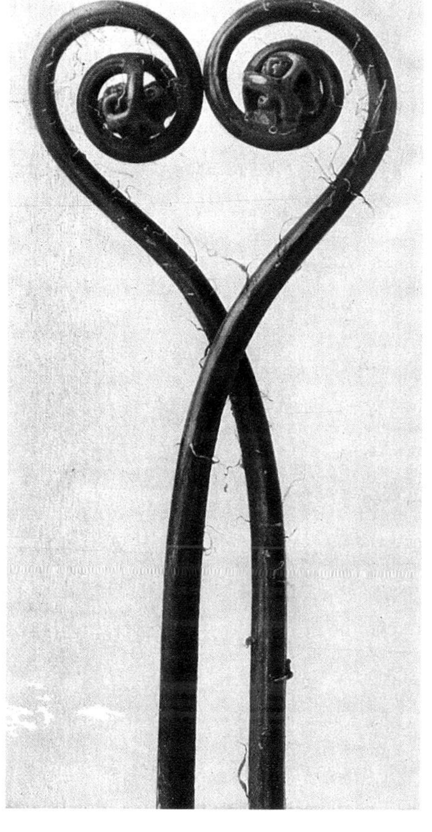

Adiantum pedatum
Maiden-hair fern
Young curled fronds magnified 8 times

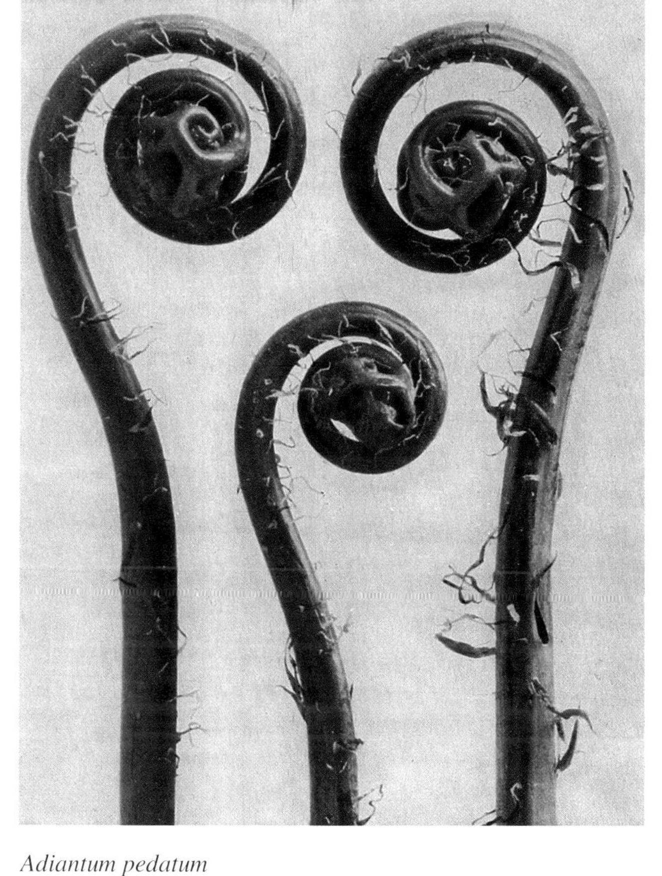

Adiantum pedatum
Maiden-hair fern
Young curled fronds magnified 12 times

Adiantum pedatum
Maiden-hair fern
Young curled fronds magnified 8 times

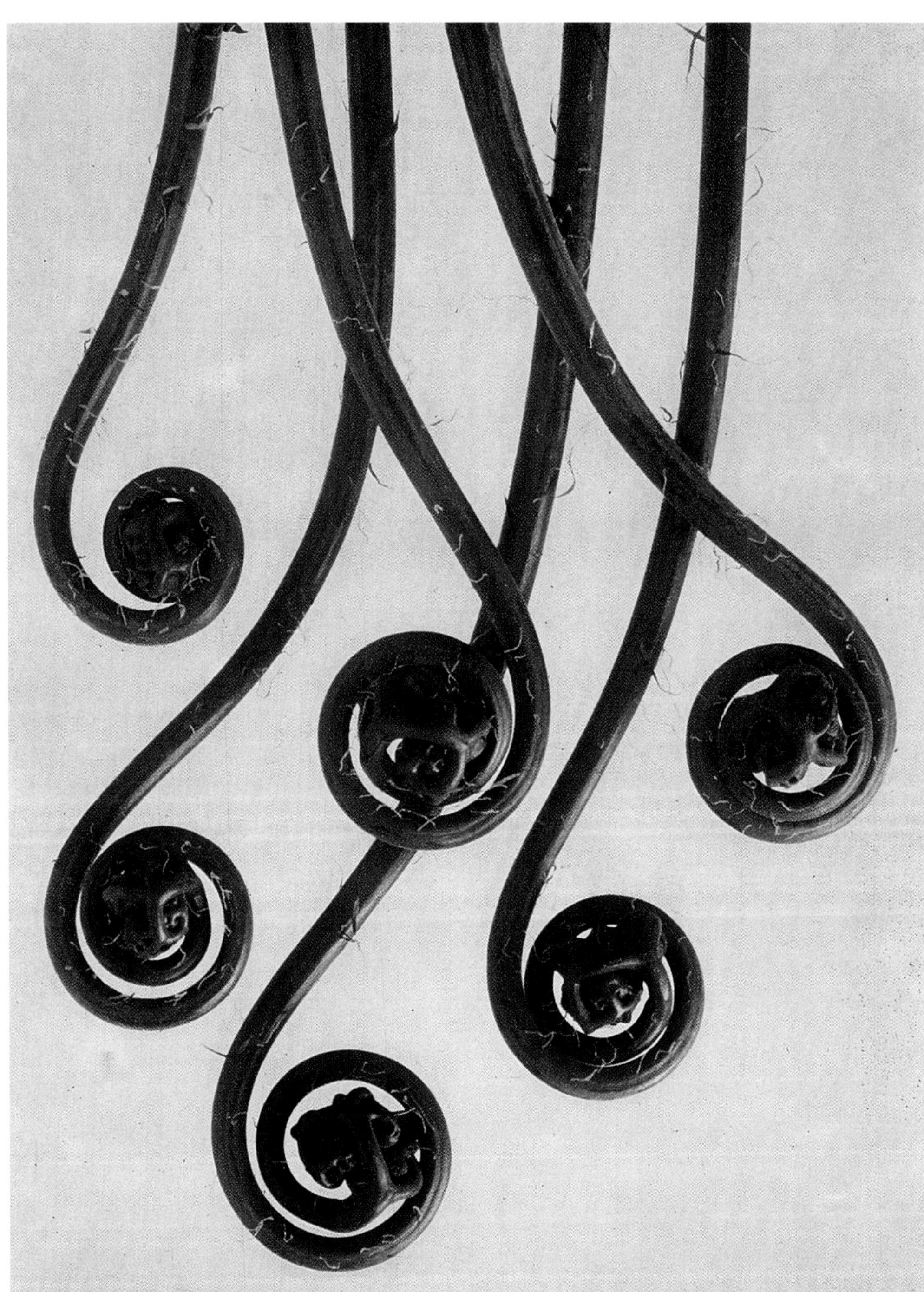

Everywhere the whole is so organized that not the slightest trace of arbitrariness remains…The conformity with natural law which is revealed is the highest form of life.
(Heinrich Wölfflin, 1915)

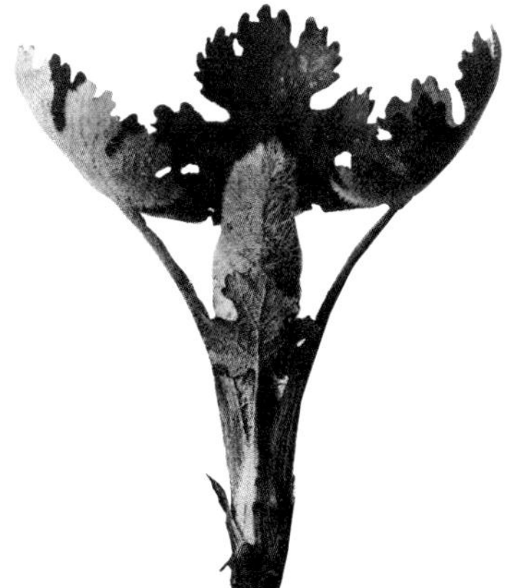

Forsythia suspensa
Tip of a forsythia twig with buds
Magnified 10 times

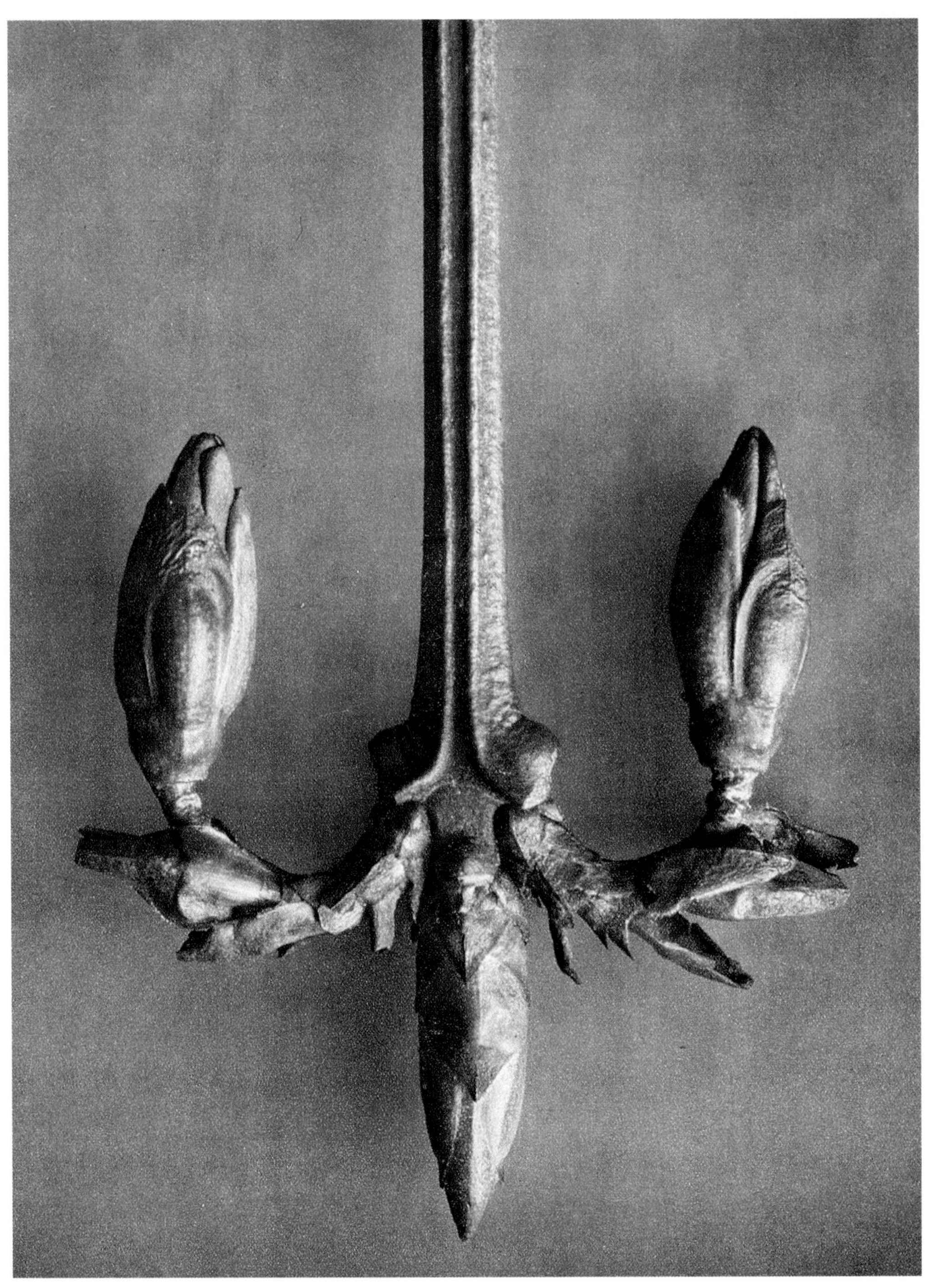

The plant is the organism in this world which is value-creative. But creating a value can really only mean the repetition of that which has become possible in an ever more sumptuary manner.

(Ernst Fuhrmann, 1935)

Aristolochia clematitis
Birthwort
Young shoot magnified 5 times

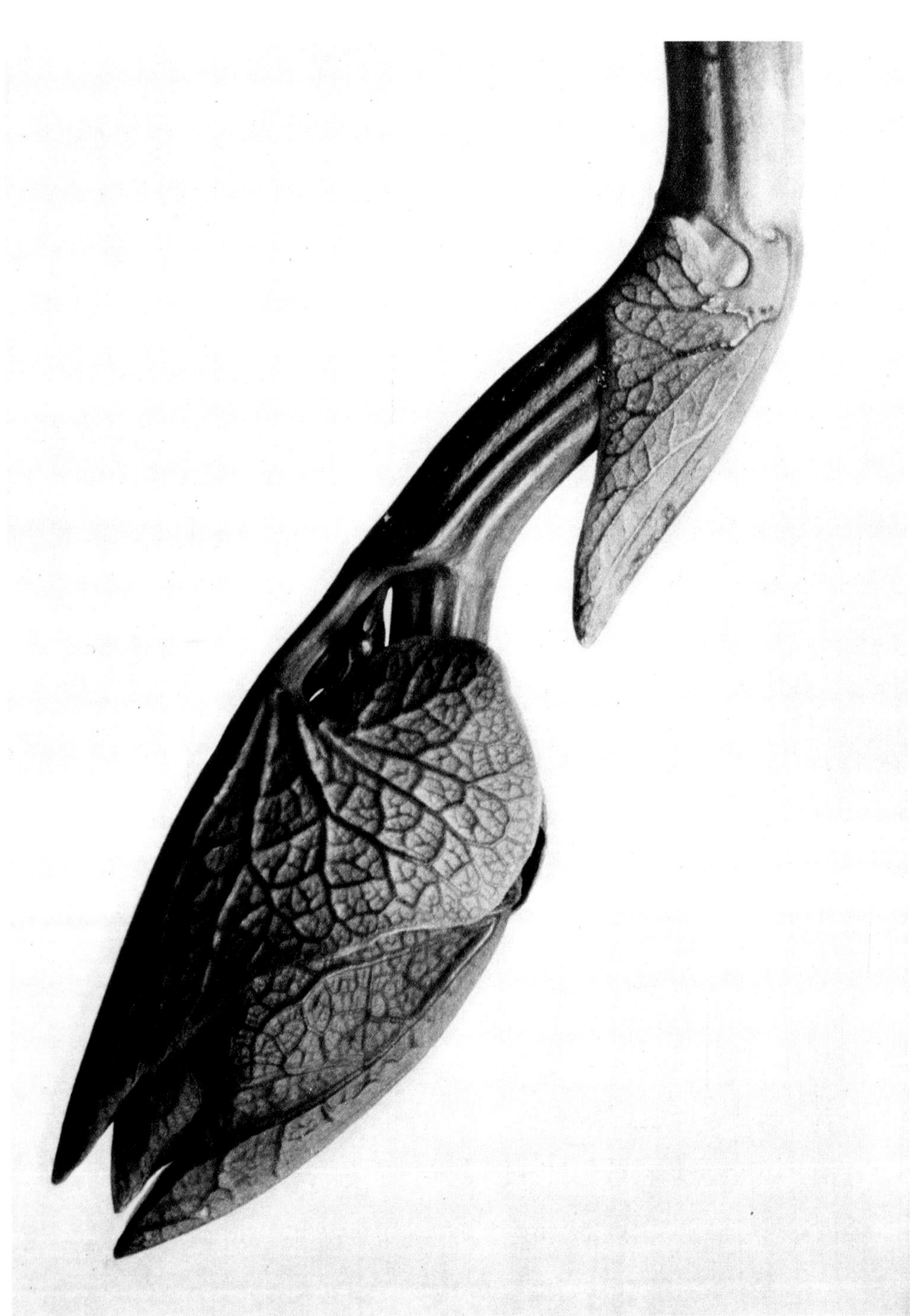

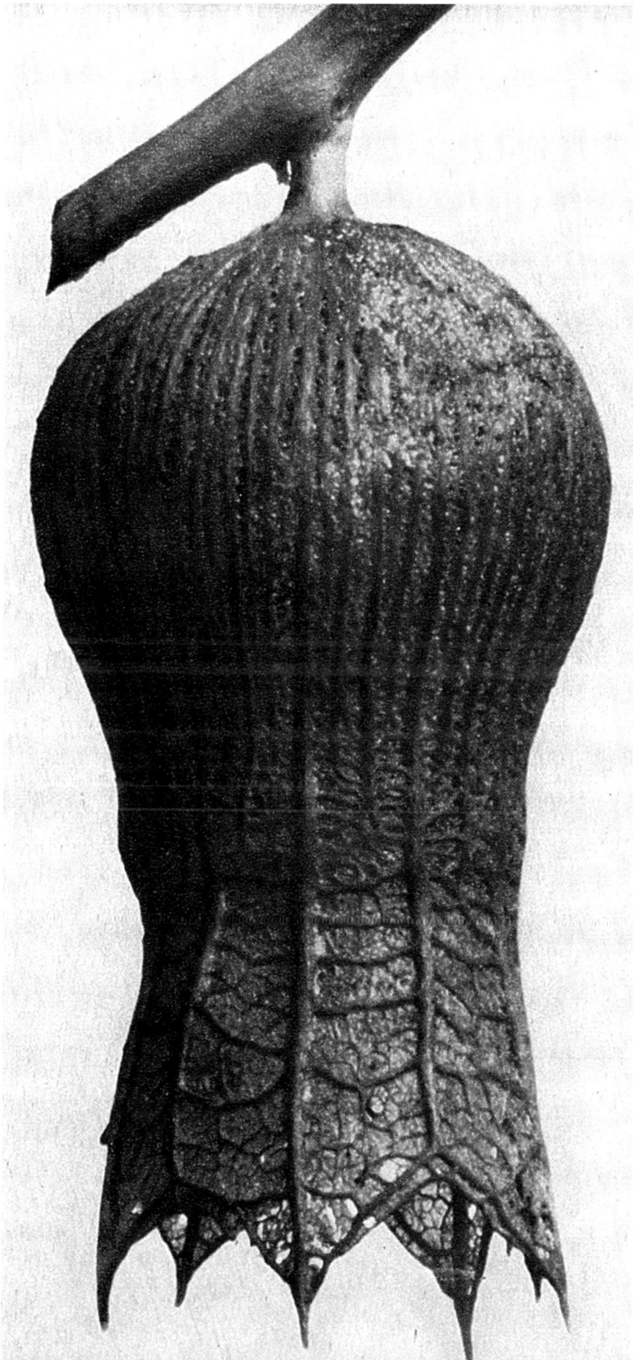

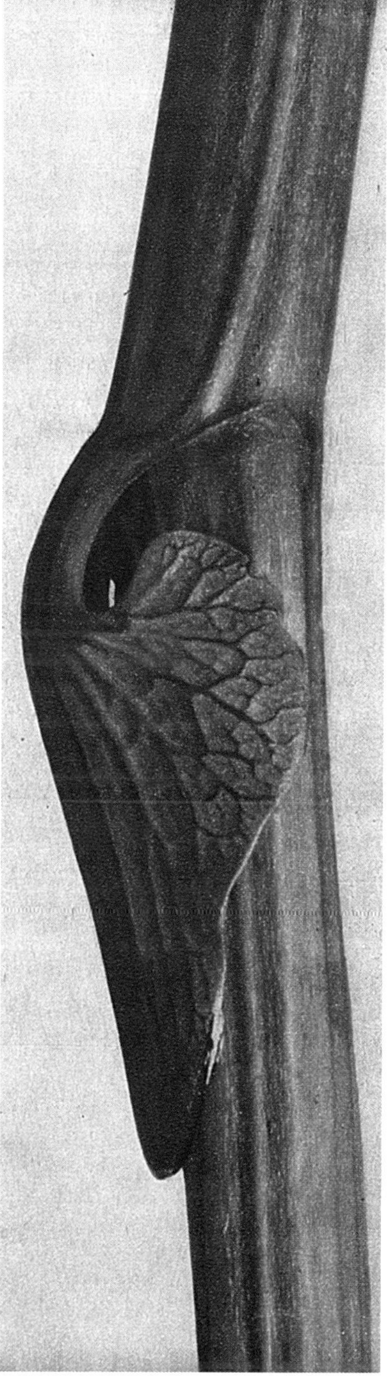

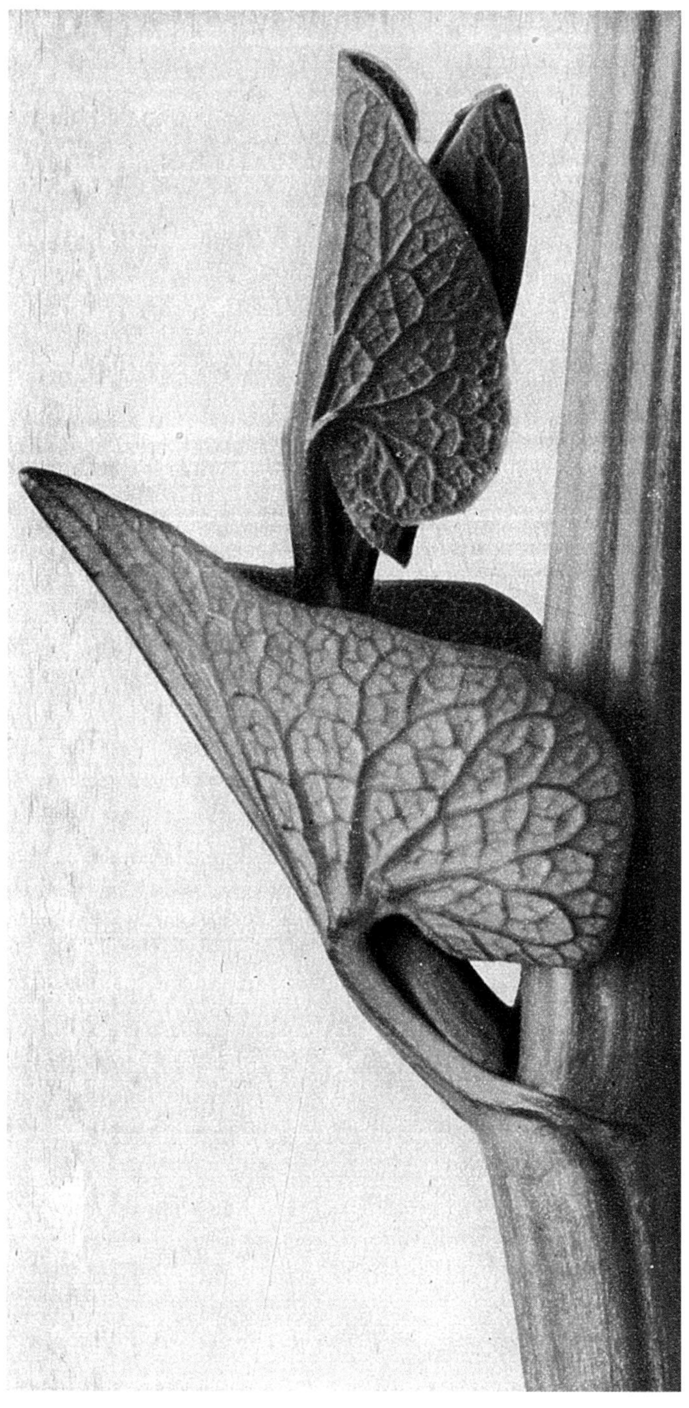

a. Aristolochia clematitis
Birthwort
Stem and leaf magnified 8 times

b. Hyoscyamus niger
Henbane
Seed capsule magnified 10 times

c. Aristolochia clematitis
Birthwort
Stem with leaf magnified 8 times

Like Lilliputians we observers wander among these gigantic plants.
(Walter Benjamin, 1929)

Taraxacum officinale
Common dandelion
Flower bud magnified 8 times

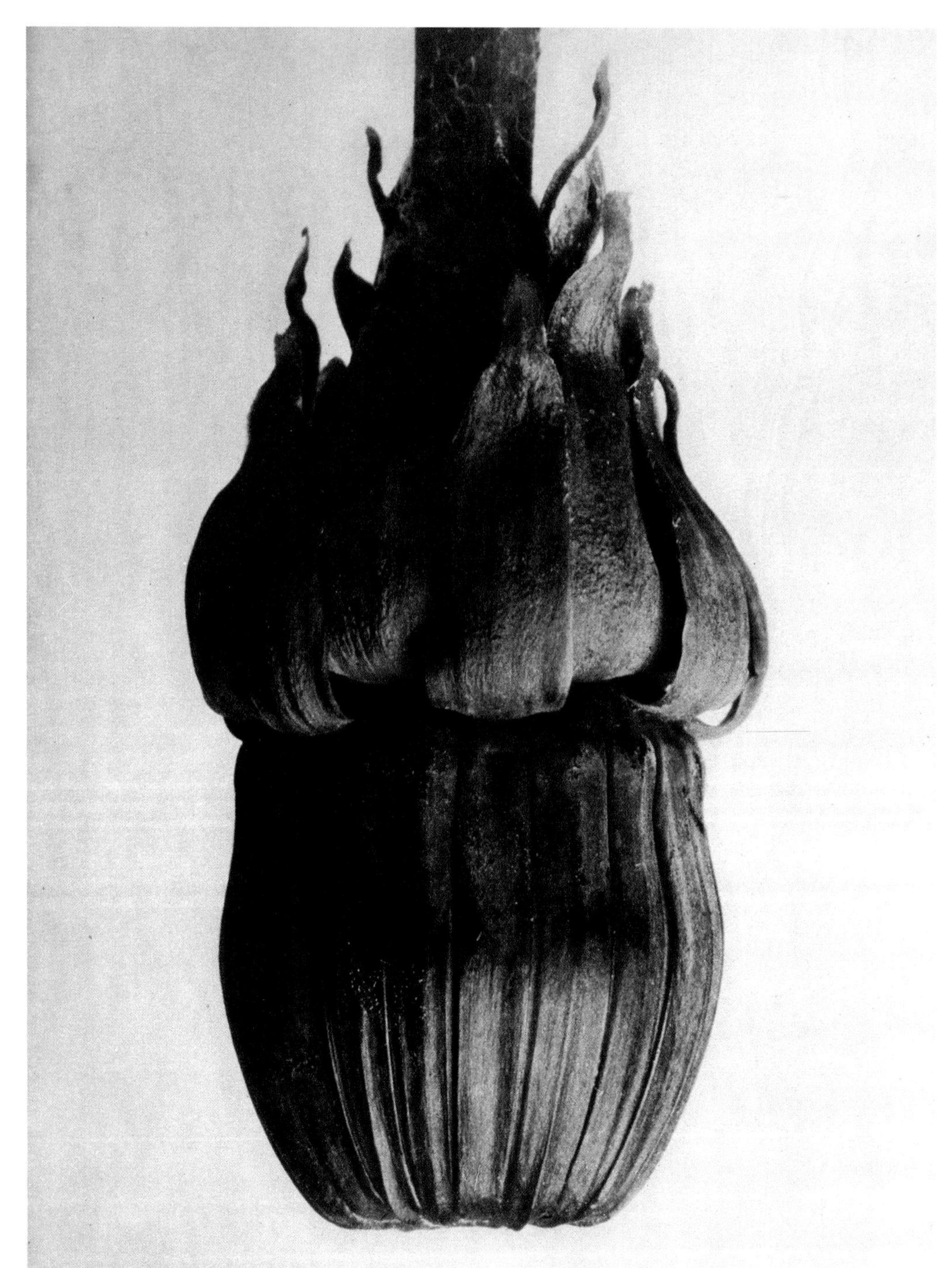

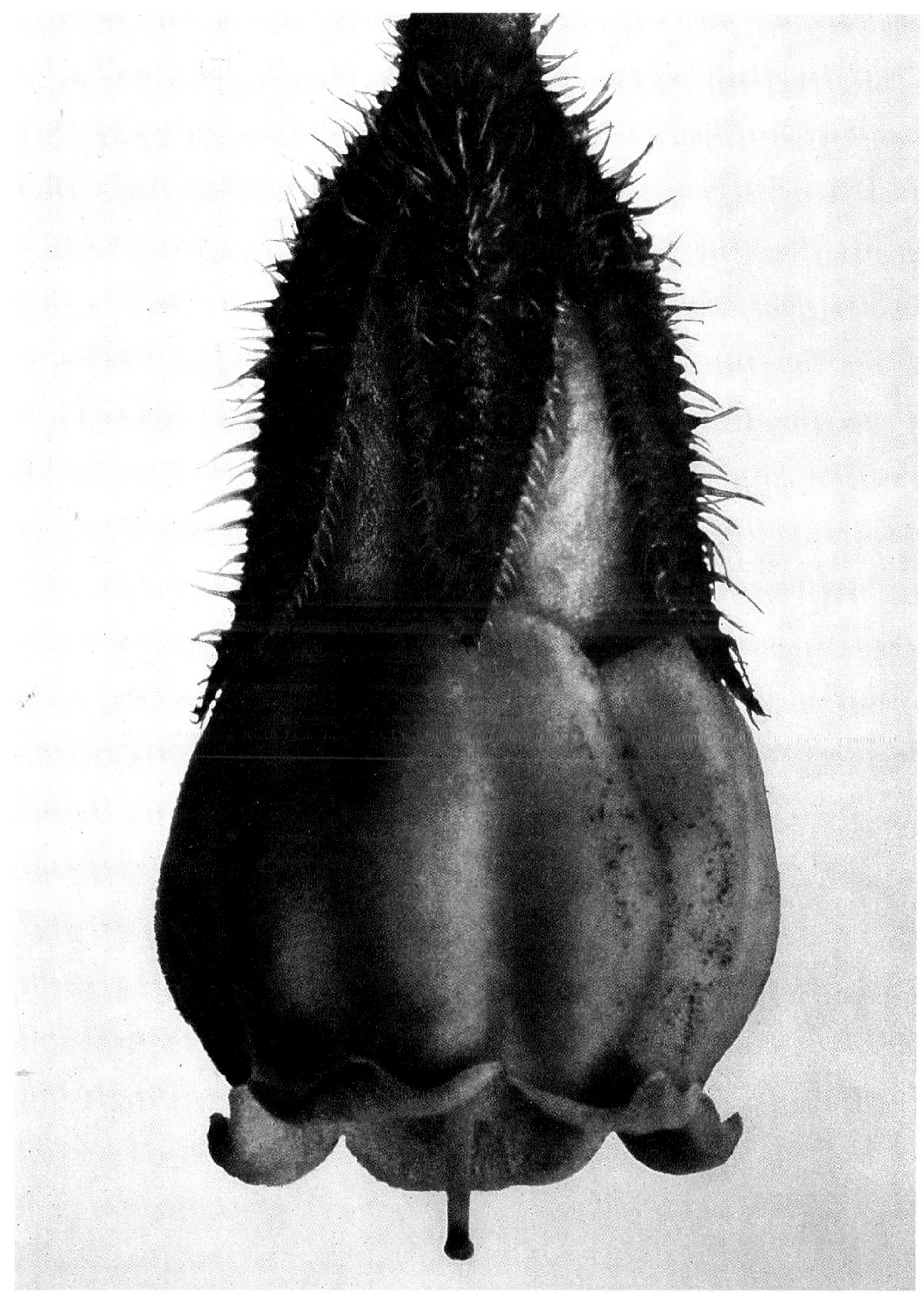

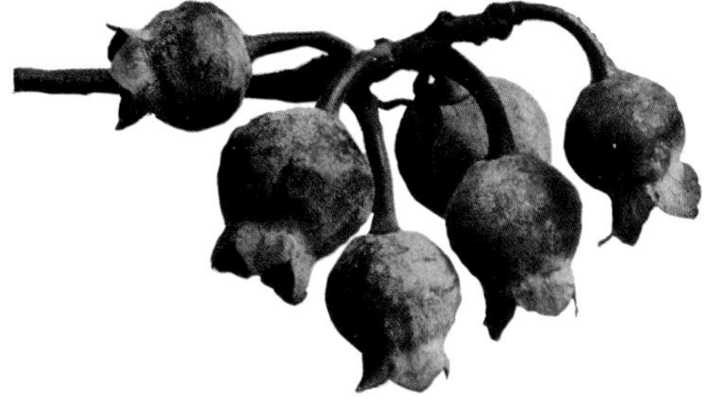

Symphytum officinale
Common comfrey
Blossom magnified 25 times

PHOTOGRAPHS ON THE FOLLOWING PAGES:

Cirsium canum
Grey thistle
Flower heads magnified 4 times

Aconitum
Monkshood
Young shoot magnified 6 times

Allium ostrowskianum
Inflorescence of a garlic species
Cluster of flowers magnified 6 times

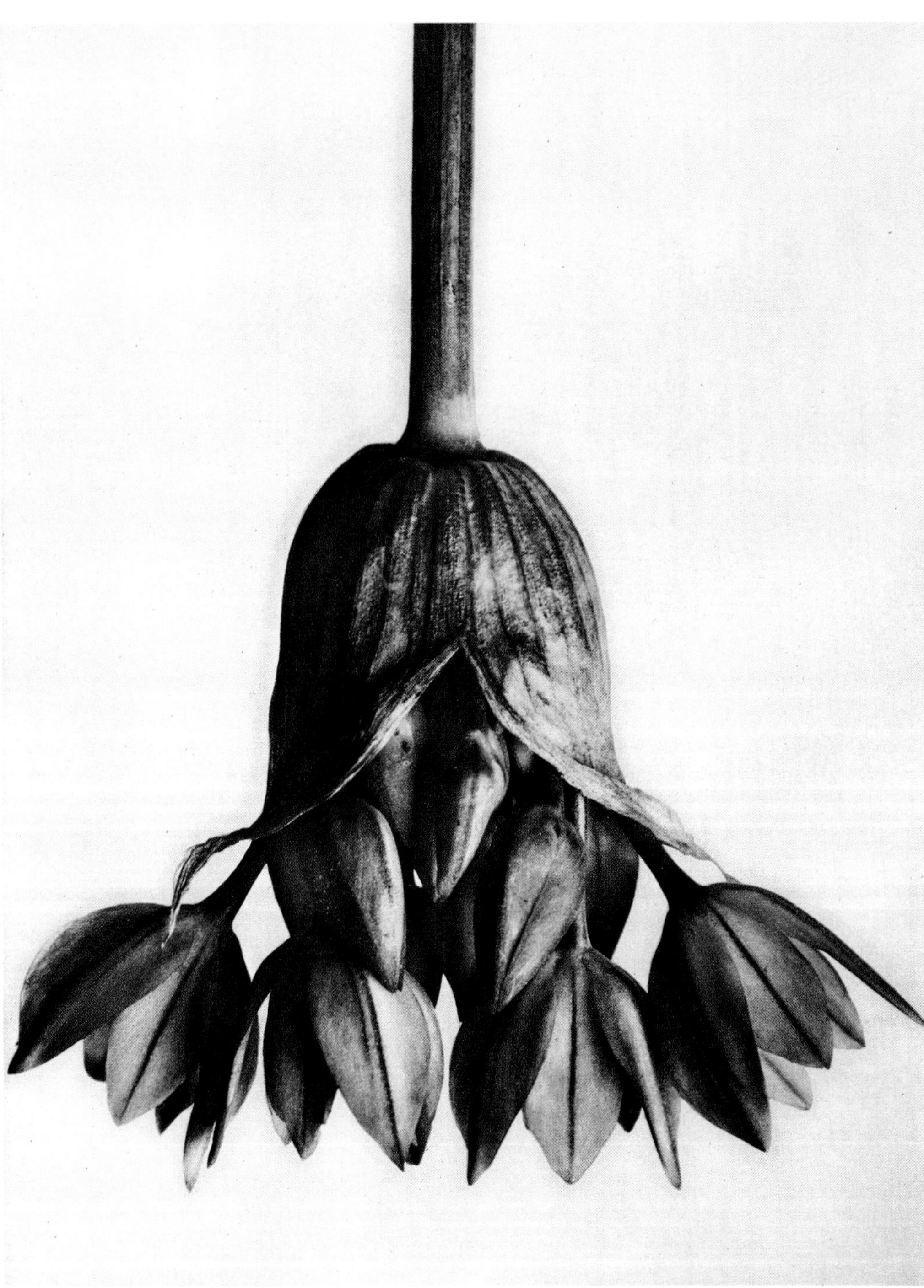

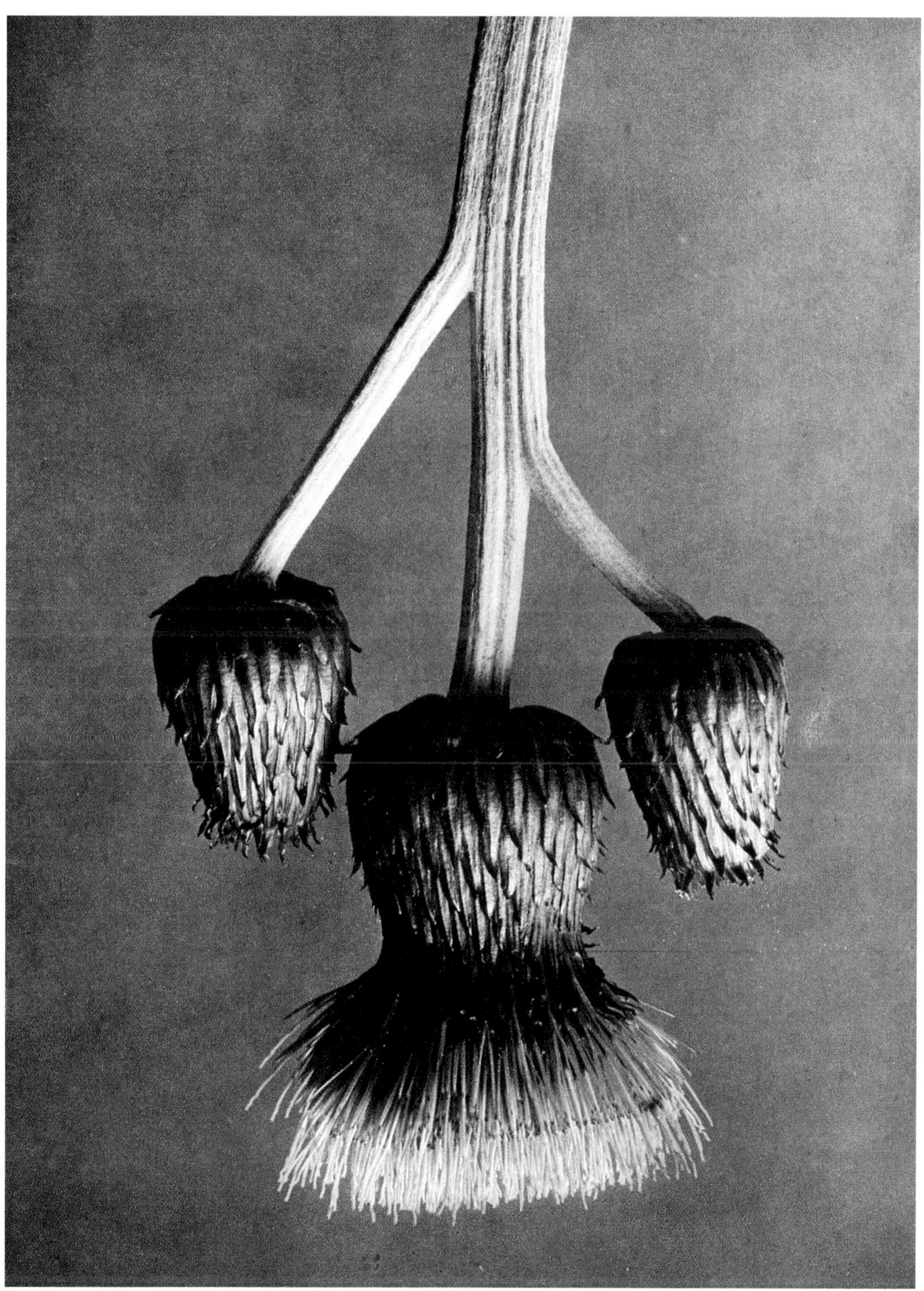

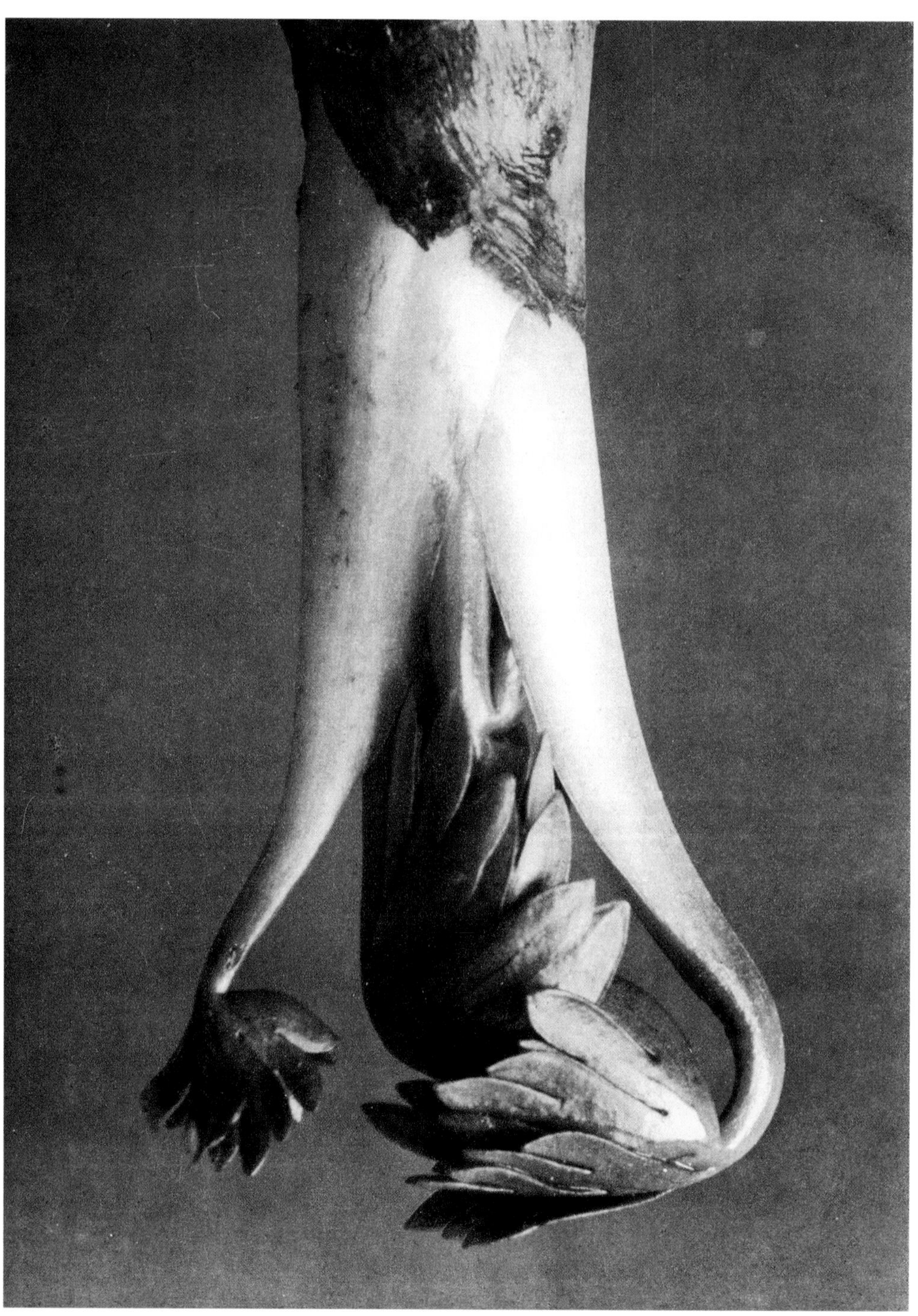

My flower documents should contribute to restoring the relationship to nature. They should reawaken a sense for nature, point out its teeming richness of form, and prompt the viewer to observe for himself the local plant world.
(Karl Blossfeldt, 1932)

Serratula nudicaulis
Sawwort
Seed heads magnified 4 times

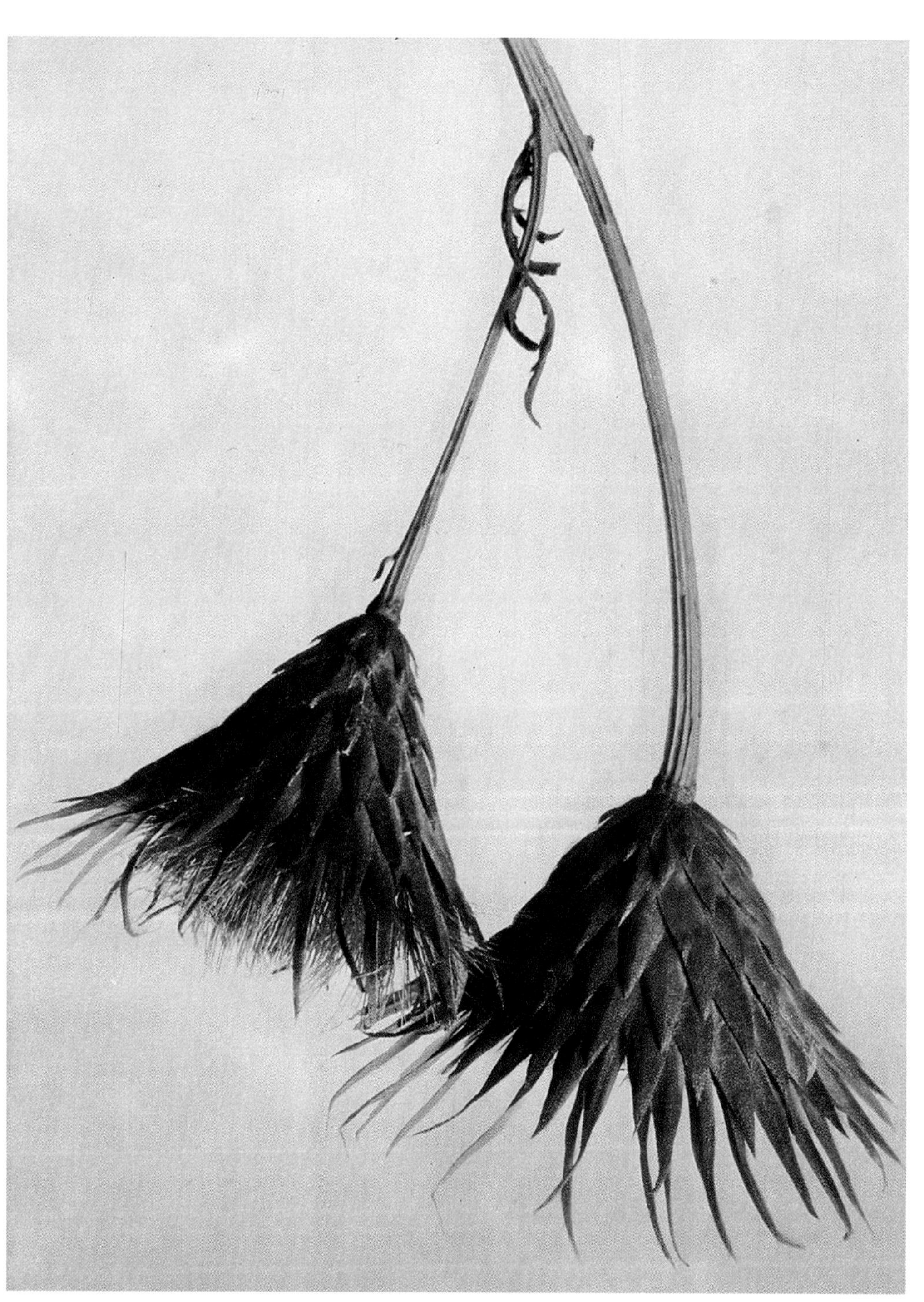

There are reasons why natural things are beautiful. Nature is above all practical, even more practical than humans. The forms of nature, developed out of necessity, are functional. And we find them beautiful precisely because…they are functional.
(Andreas Feininger, 1955)

Abutilon
Flowering maple
Seed capsules magnified 6 times

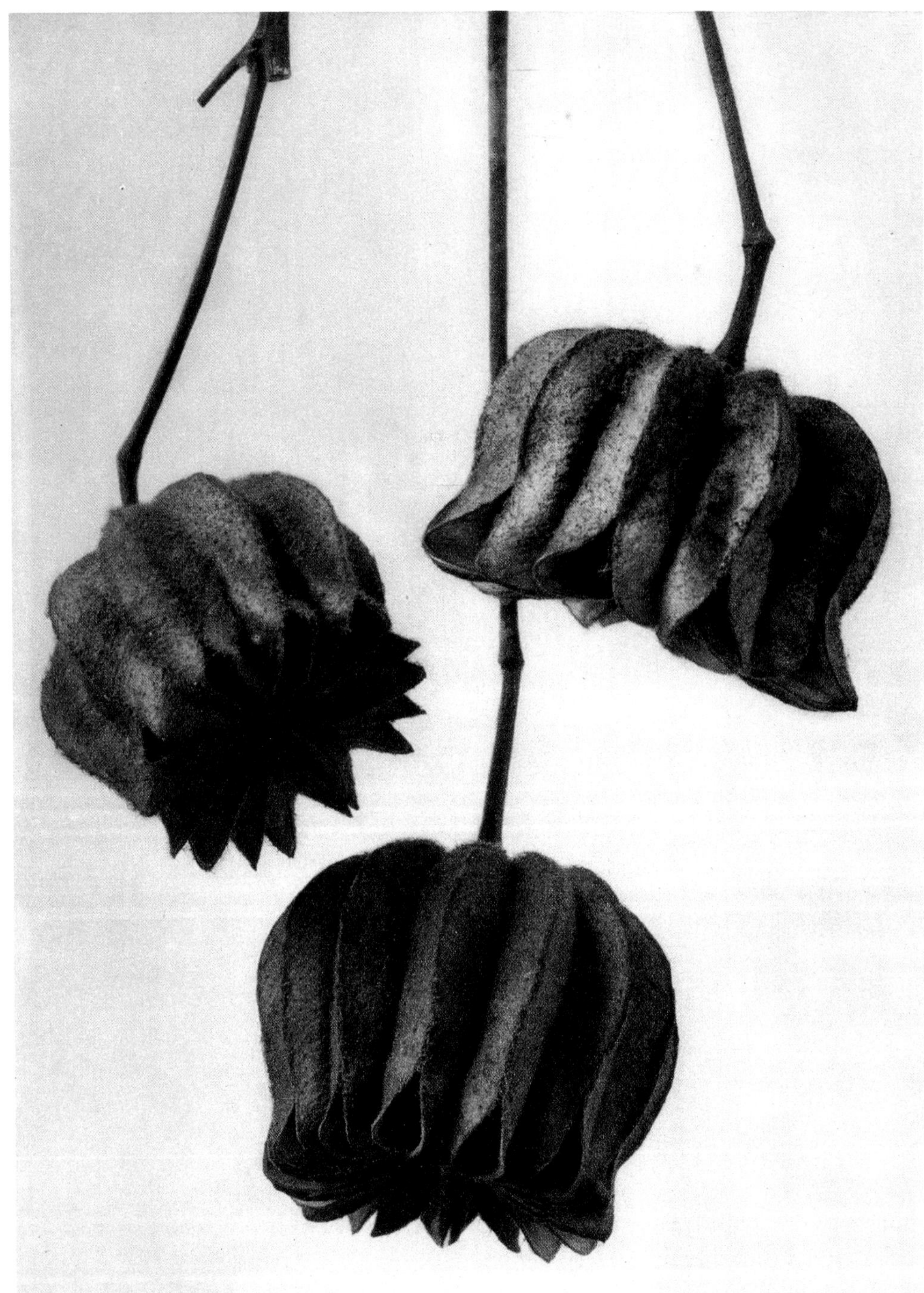

PHOTOGRAPHS ON THE FOLLOWING PAGES:
Campanula alliarifolia
Bell-flower
Flower magnified 10 times

Azorina vidalii
Bell-flower (with petals removed)
Magnified 10 times

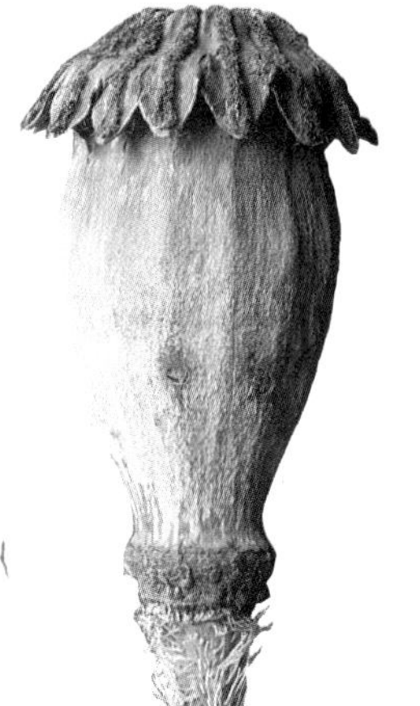

Papaver
Poppy
Magnified 6 times

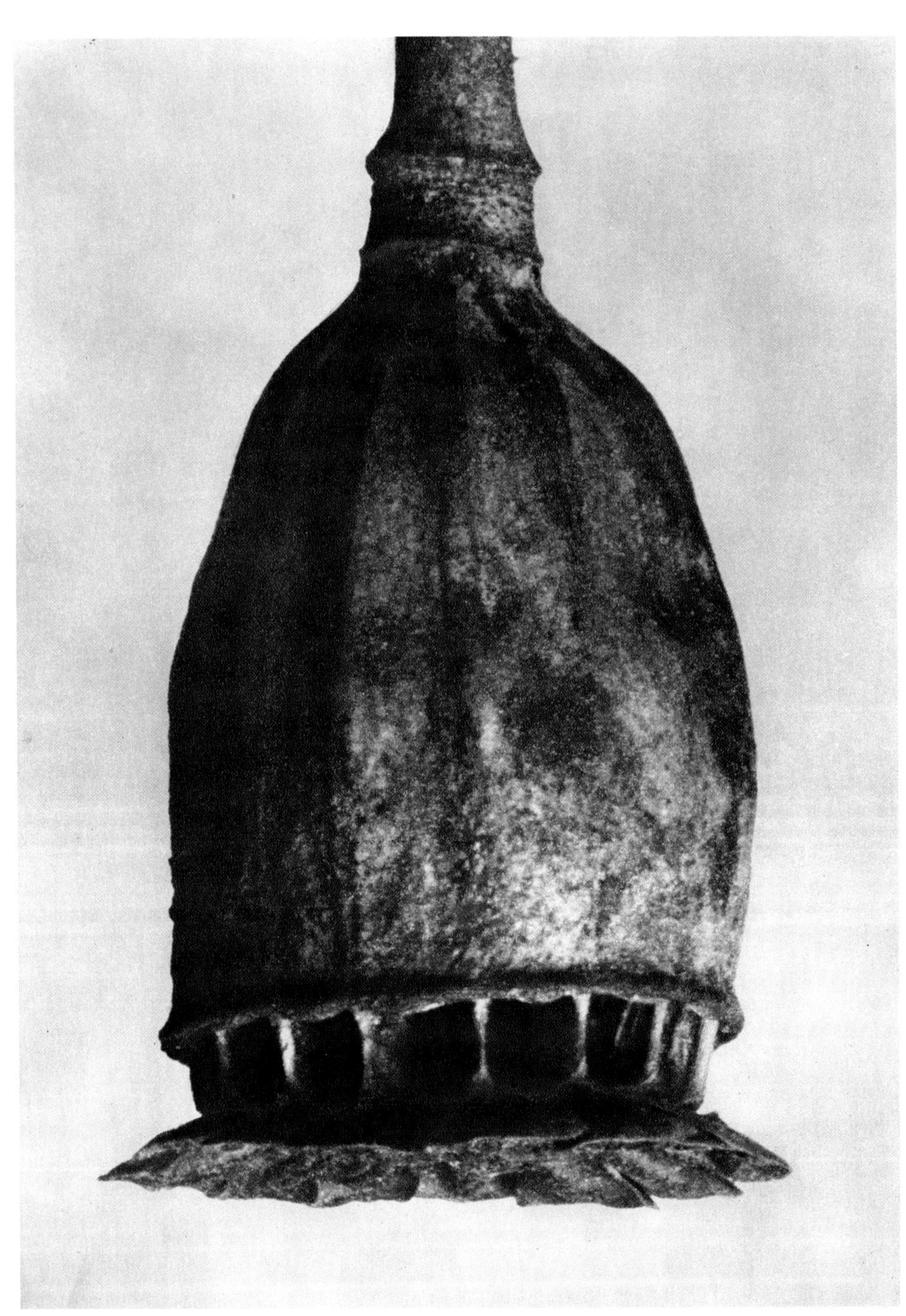

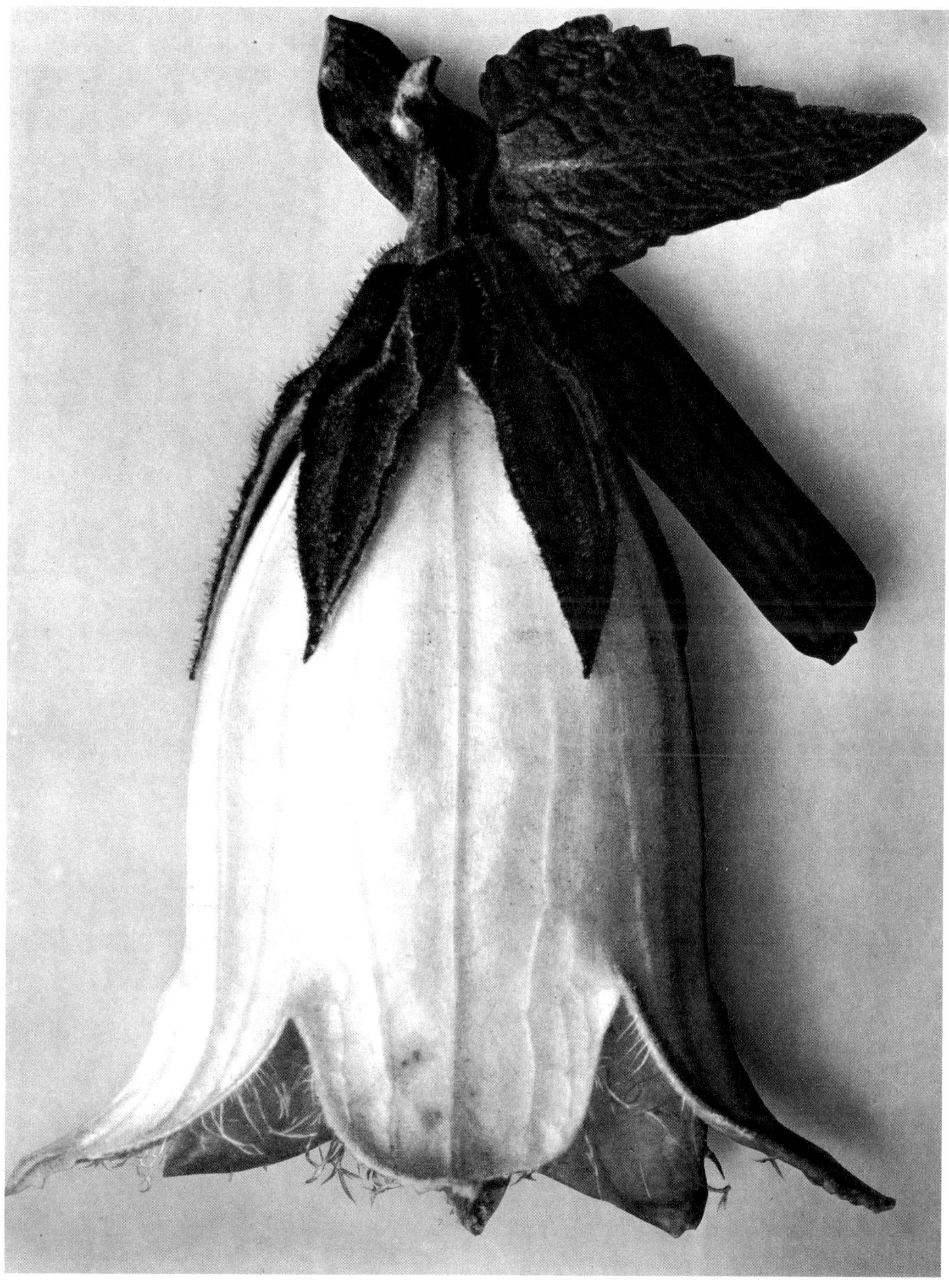

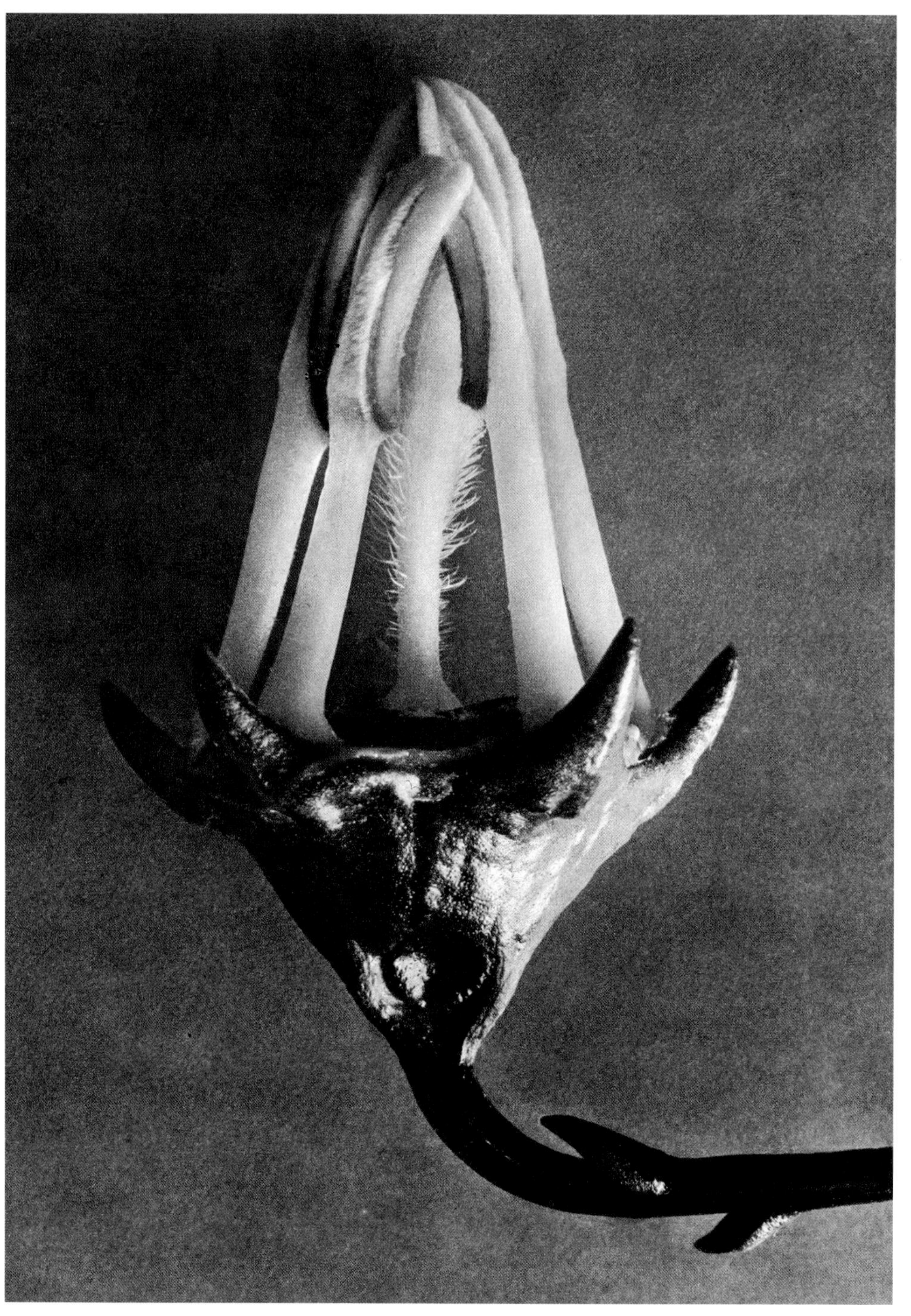

PHOTOGRAPHS ON THE FOLLOWING PAGES:

Hordeum distichon
Barley
Magnified 4 times

Uniola latifolia
Fescue grass
Spikelets magnified 2.5 times

Achillea clypeolata
Yarrow
Cyme magnified 15 times

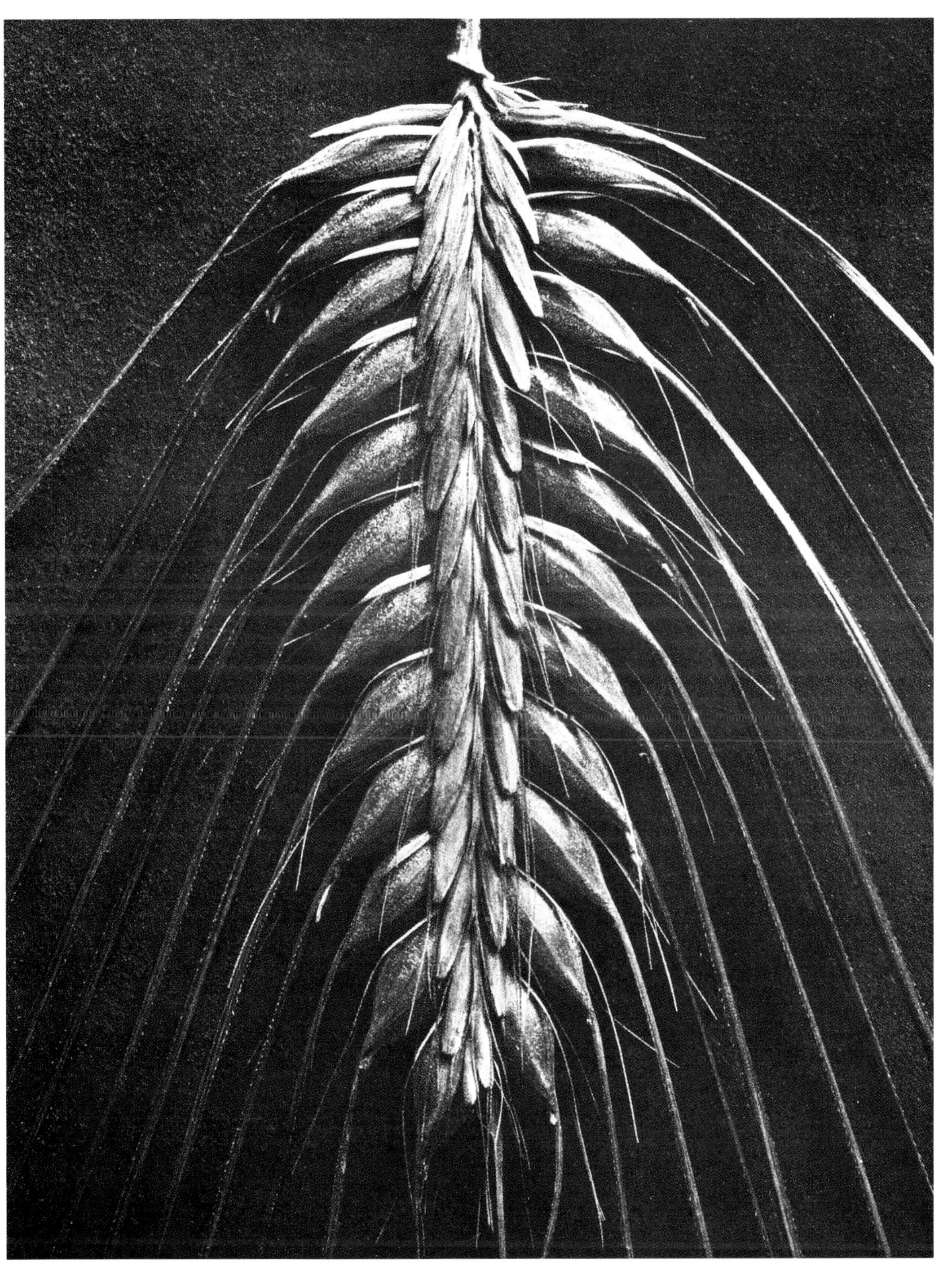

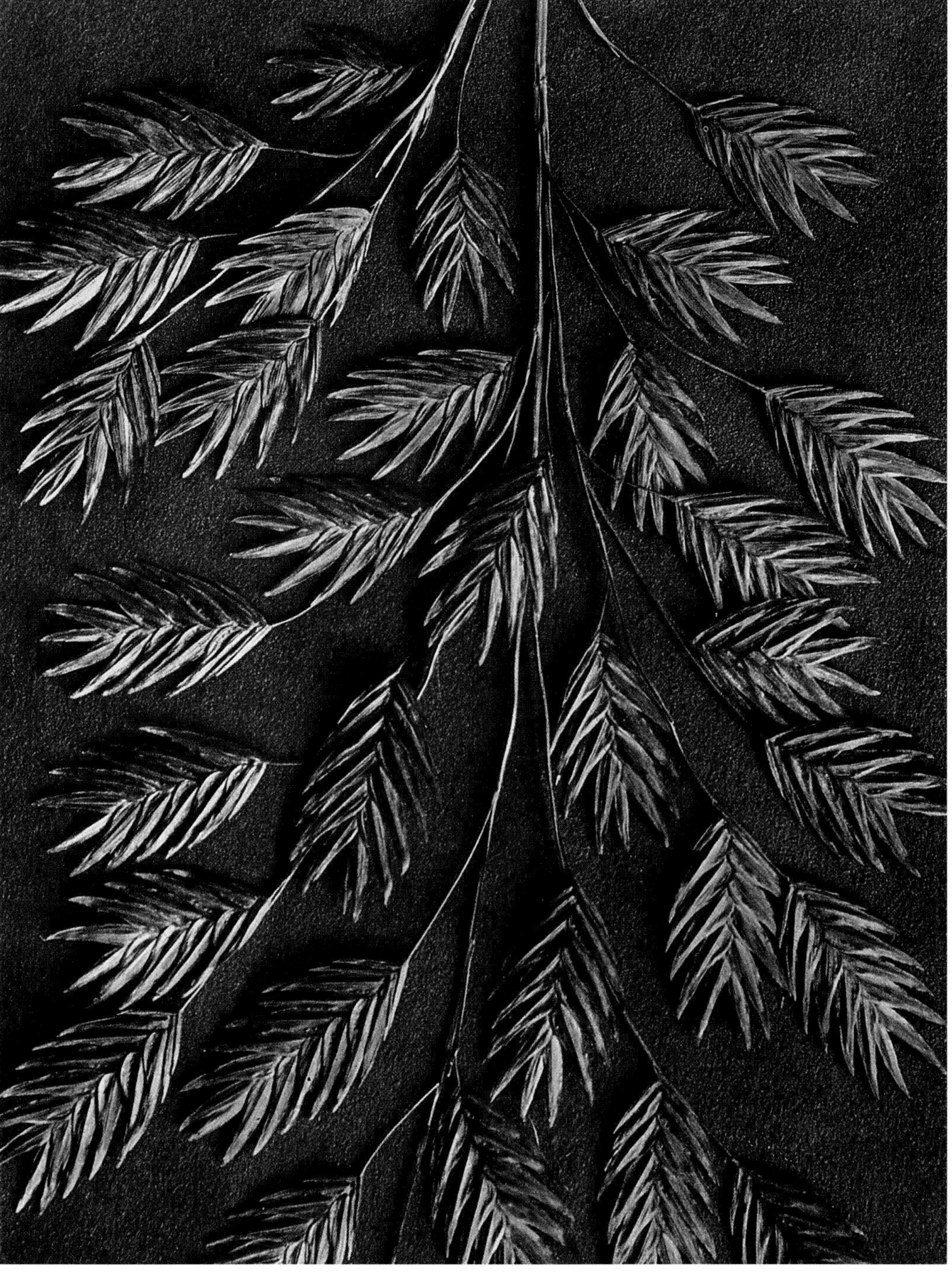

PHOTOGRAPHS ON THE FOLLOWING PAGES:

a. Passiflora
Passion-flower
Magnified 4 times

b. Cobaea scandens
Calyx
Flower bud magnified 4 times

c. Epimedium musschianum
Barrenwort
Blossom magnified 24 times

d. Dianthus plumarius
Common pink
Magnified 8 times

e. Cobaea scandens
Calyx
Magnified 4 times

Laserpitum siler
Laserwort
Part of a fertilizing cluster magnified 4 times

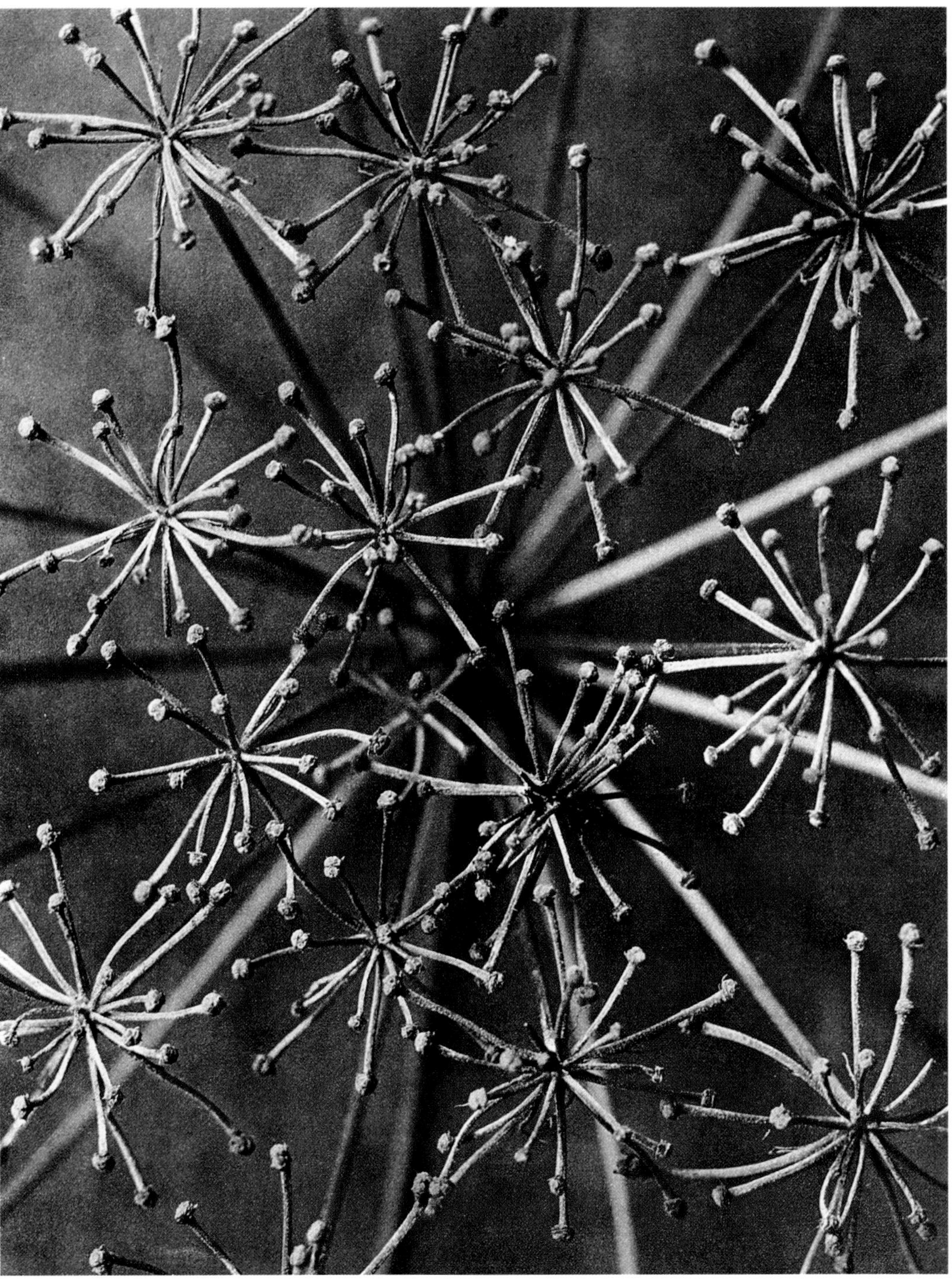

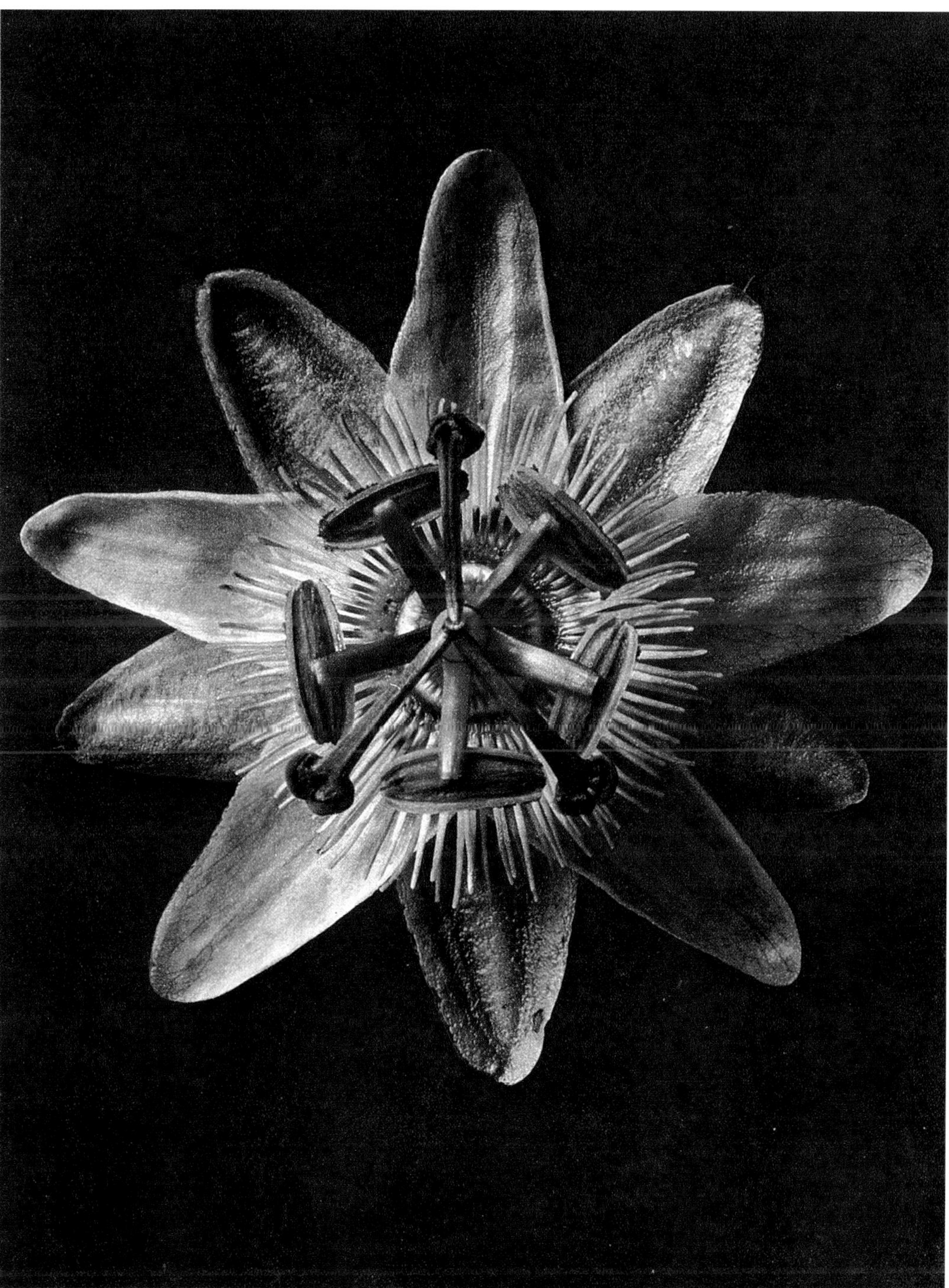

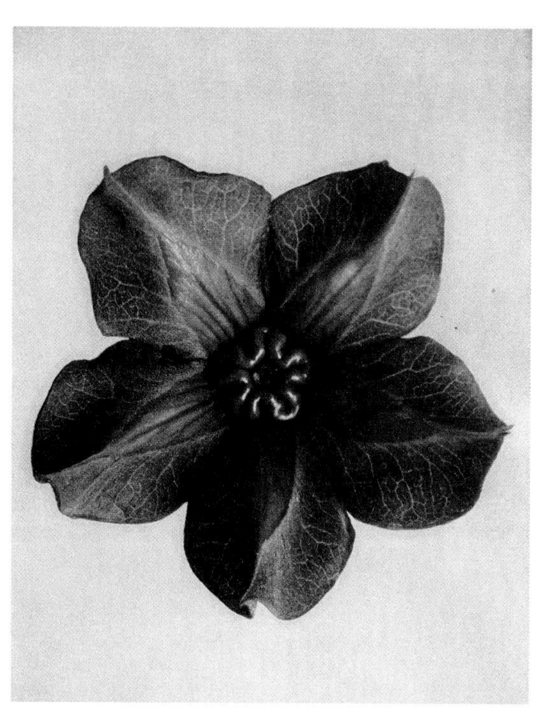
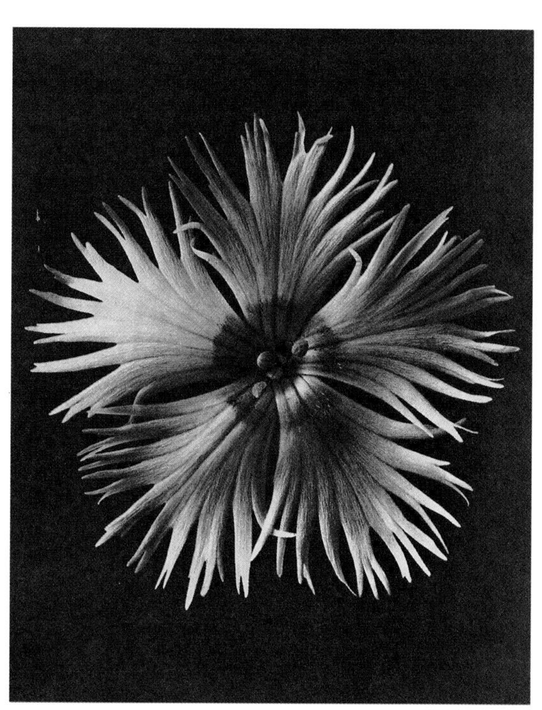
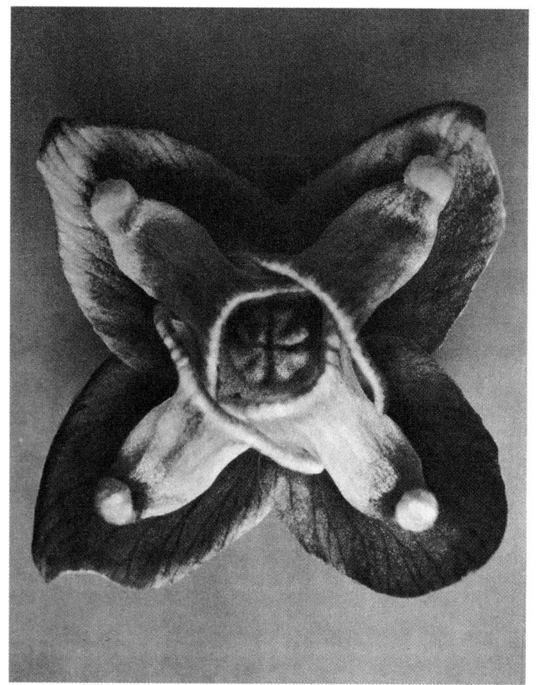
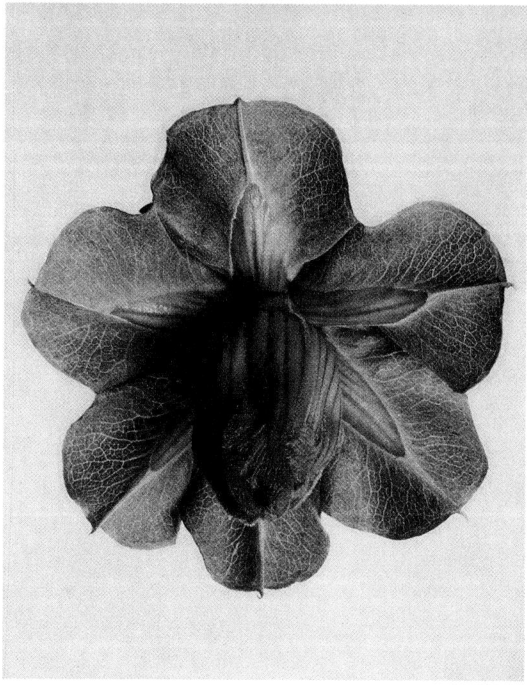

If art has ever consisted in setting signs in which a decisive stand towards reality clearly articulates itself and in which there is an emphatic prospect of a better reality, then Blossfeldt is an artist.
(Klaus Honnef, 1976)

Tilia americana
American lime
a. Flower magnified 9 times
b. Flowers magnified 6 times

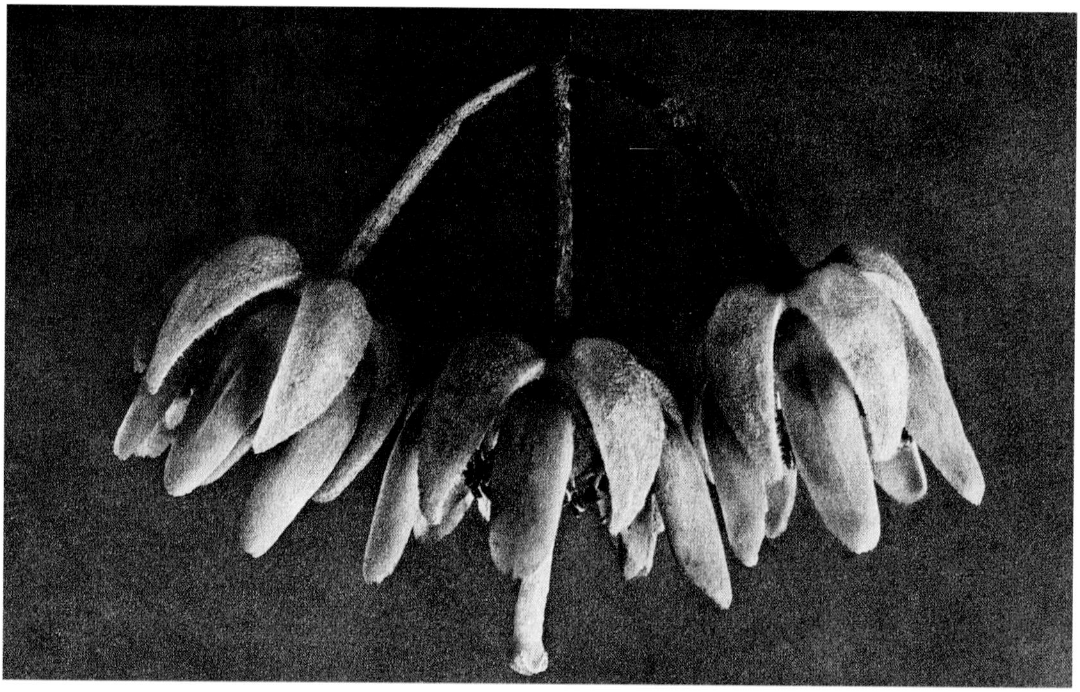

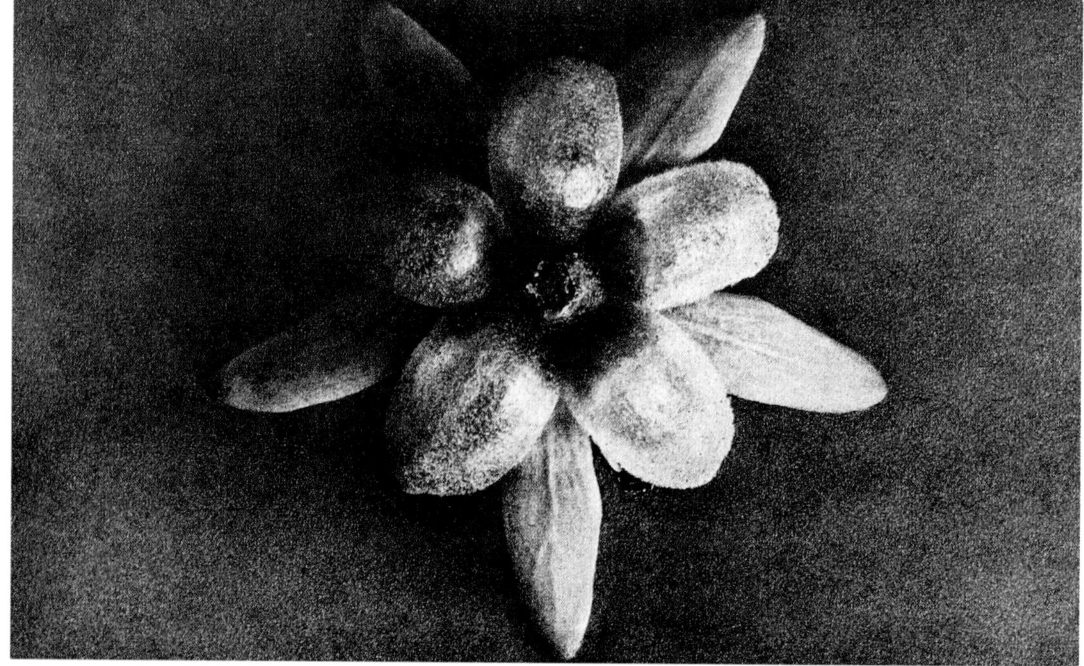

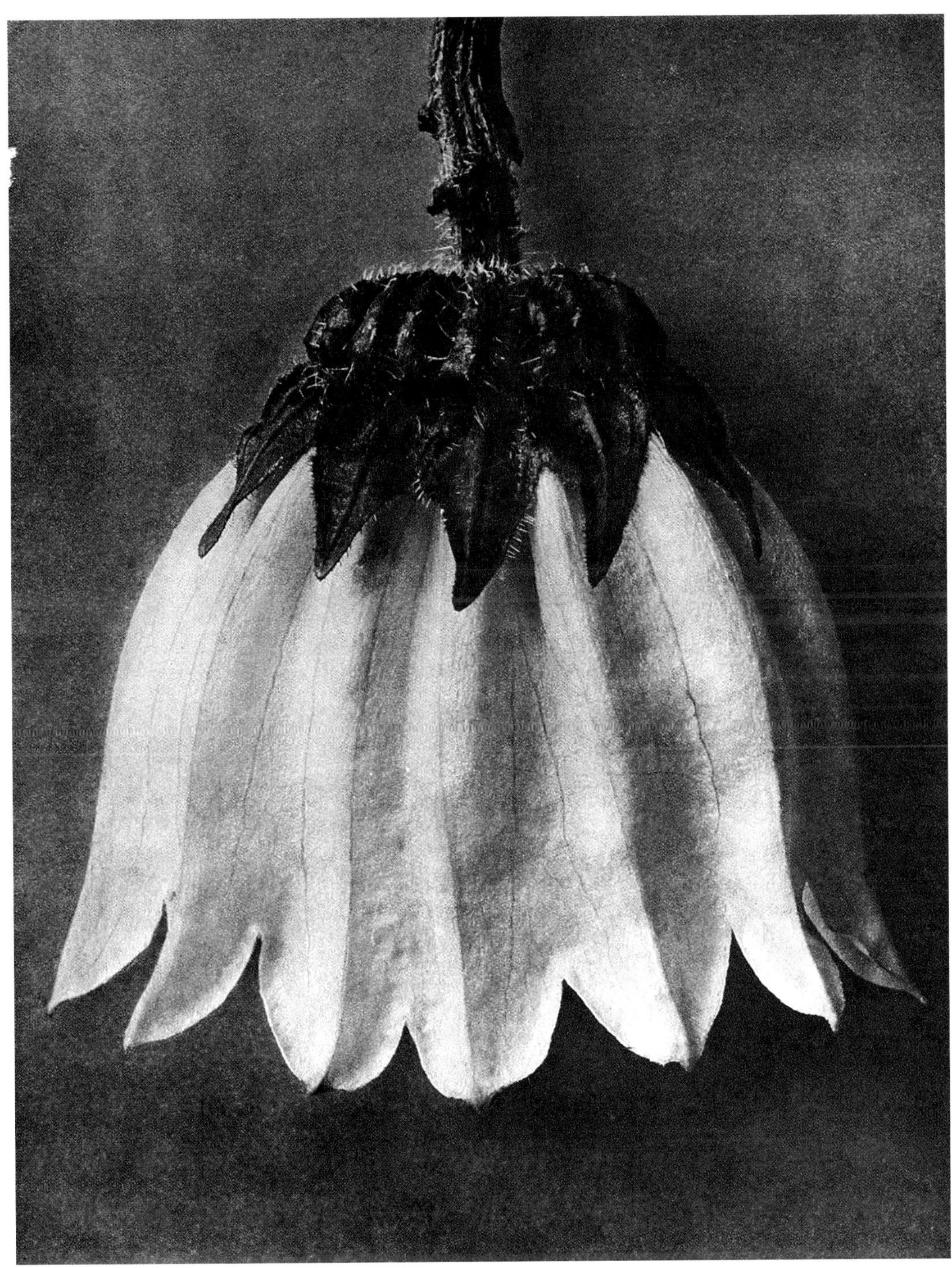

PHOTOGRAPHS ON THE FOLLOWING PAGES:
Eryngium maritimum
Sea holly
Spathes with flower head magnified 4 times

Blumenbachia hieronymi (Loasaceae)
Opened seed capsule magnified 8 times

In 'nature'... new genetic information is created through error and through the faulty transmission of information from one carrier to another. The vast majority of information produced in this way is meaningless nonsense and only a tiny number of such mutations lead to new species and are responsible for biological development. That means that 'nature' (whatever that may be) is extremely stupid, and what we so admire about plants is precisely this incredible stupidity.
(Vilém Flusser, 1985)

Campanula medium
Bell-flower
Magnified 5 times

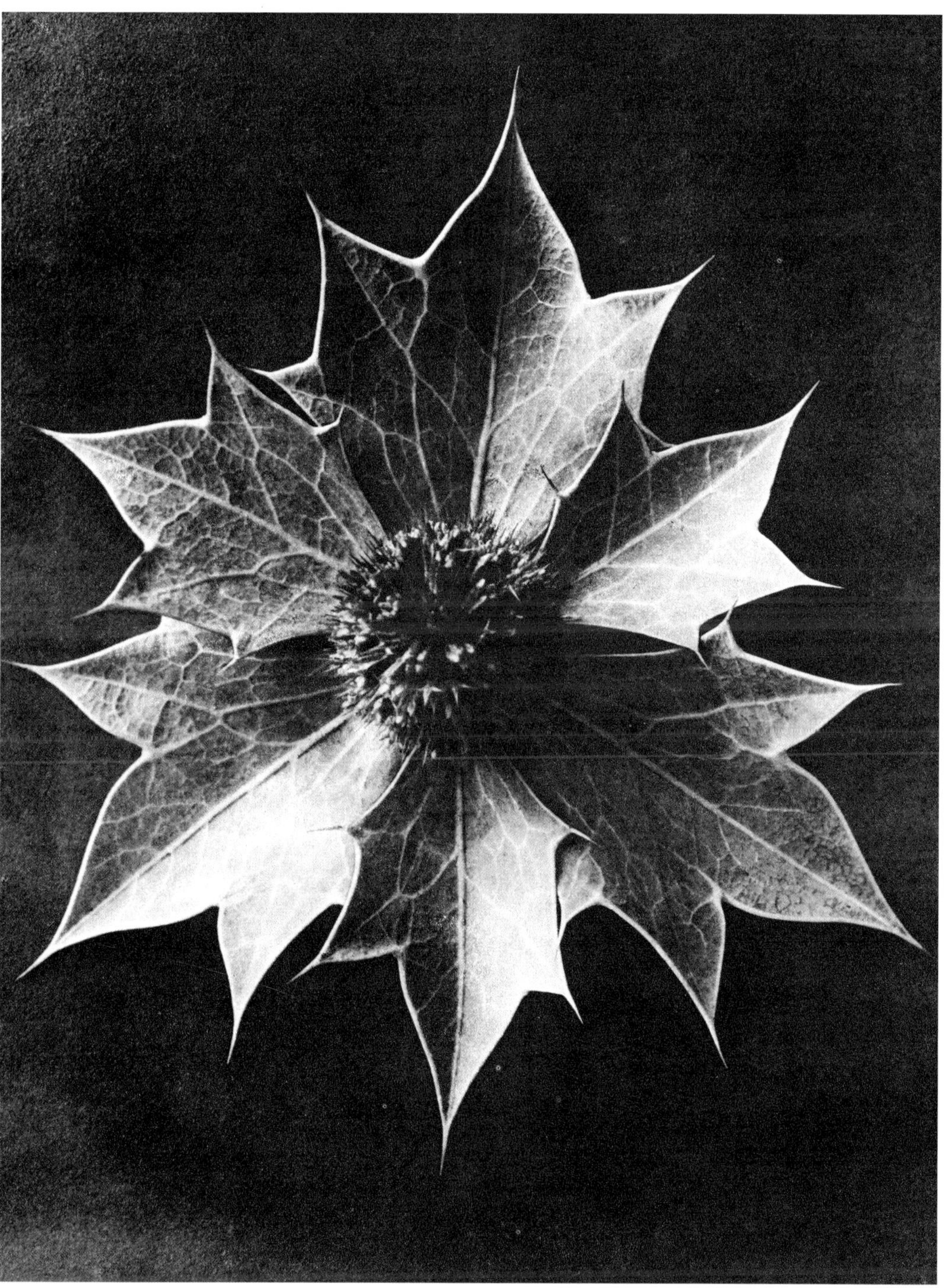

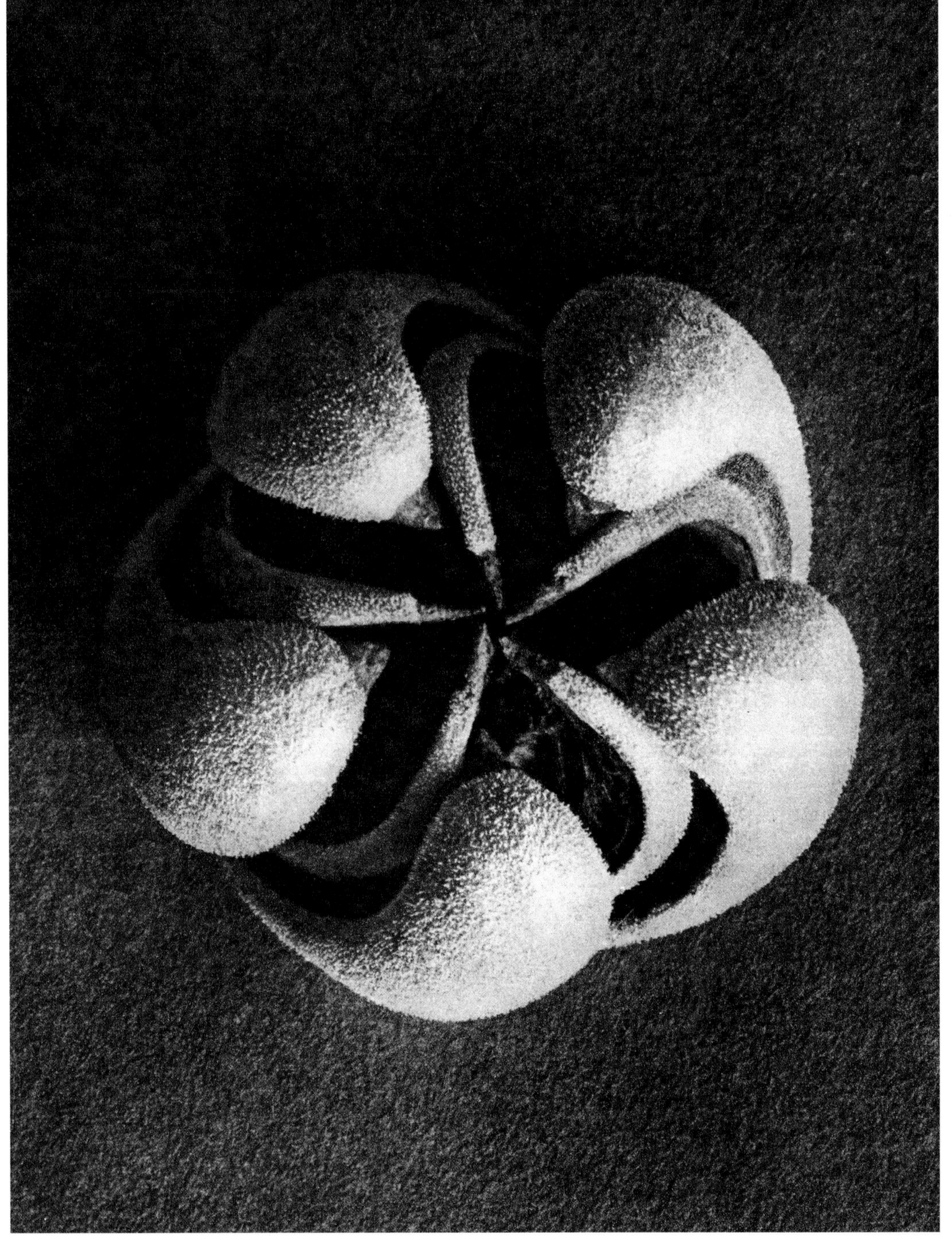

Blossfeldt was no camera enthusiast. How could he otherwise have put up with this monotony? He was a plant-lover.
(Gert Mattenklott, 1981)

Impatiens glandulifera
Indian balsam
Stem with branches, life-sized

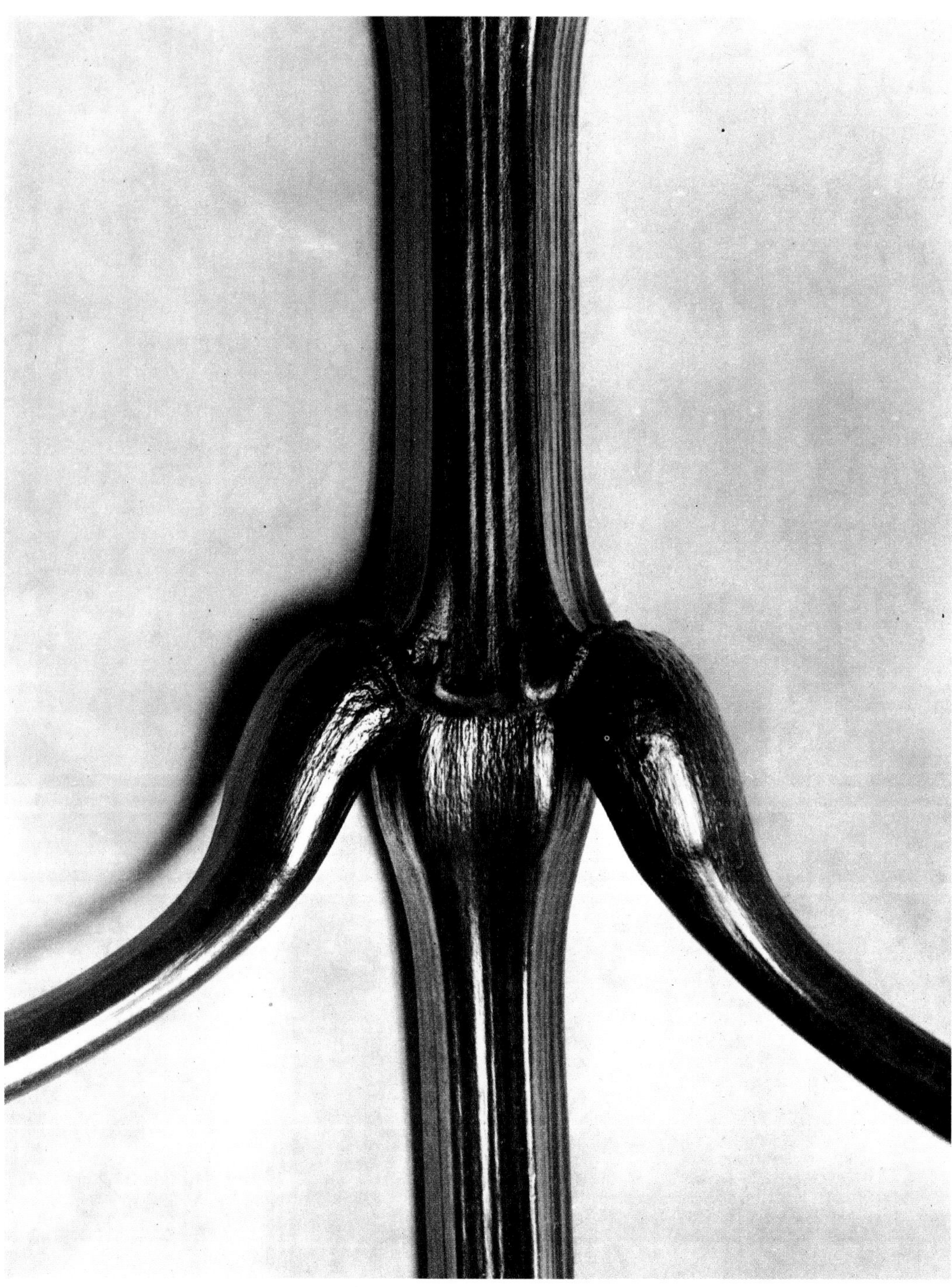

PHOTOGRAPHS ON THE FOLLOWING PAGES:

Dipsacus fullonum
Common teasel
Flower head magnified 6 times

Papaver orientale
Oriental poppy
Flower bud

Trollius ledebourii
Globeflower
Fruit magnified 10 times

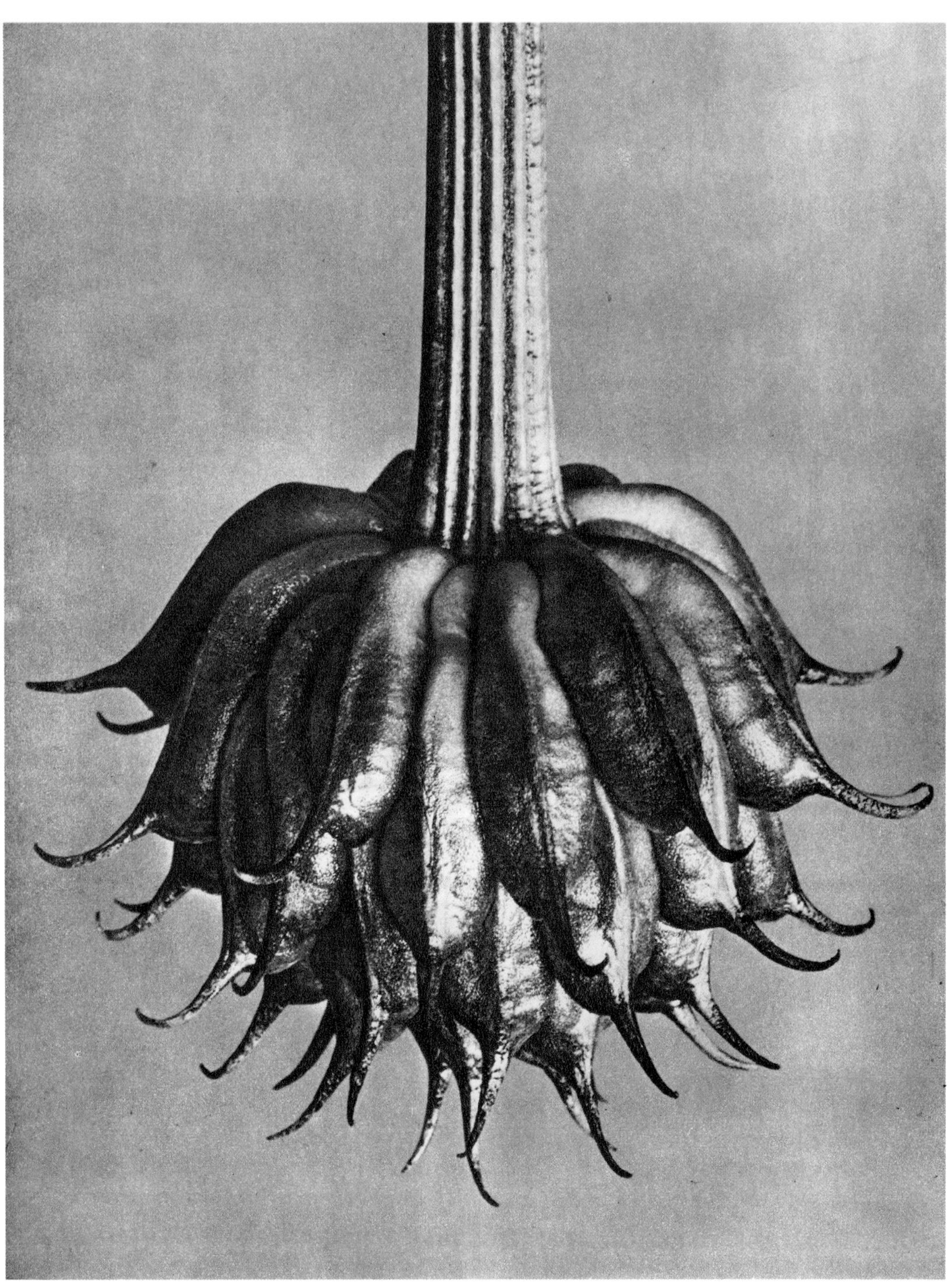

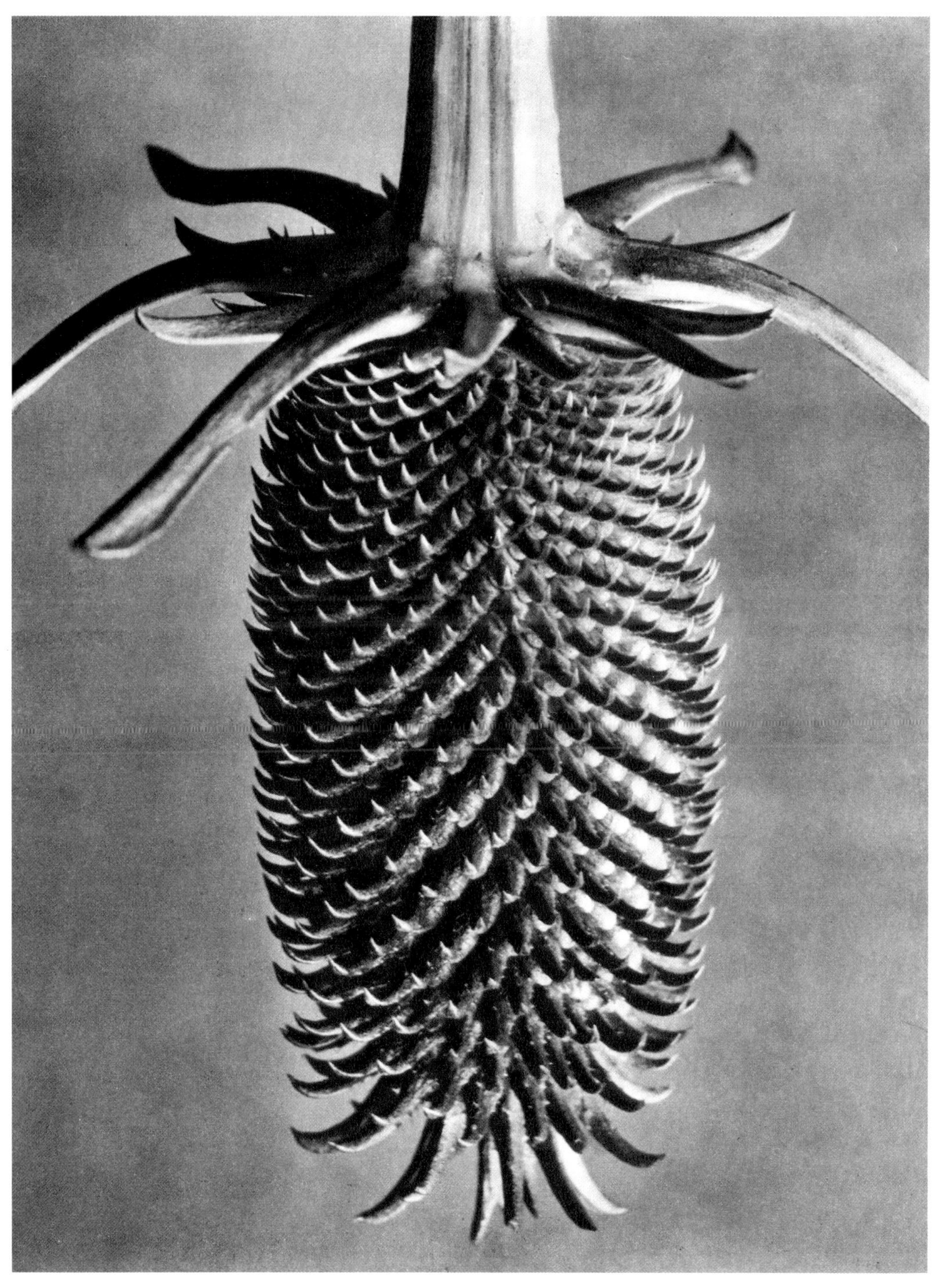

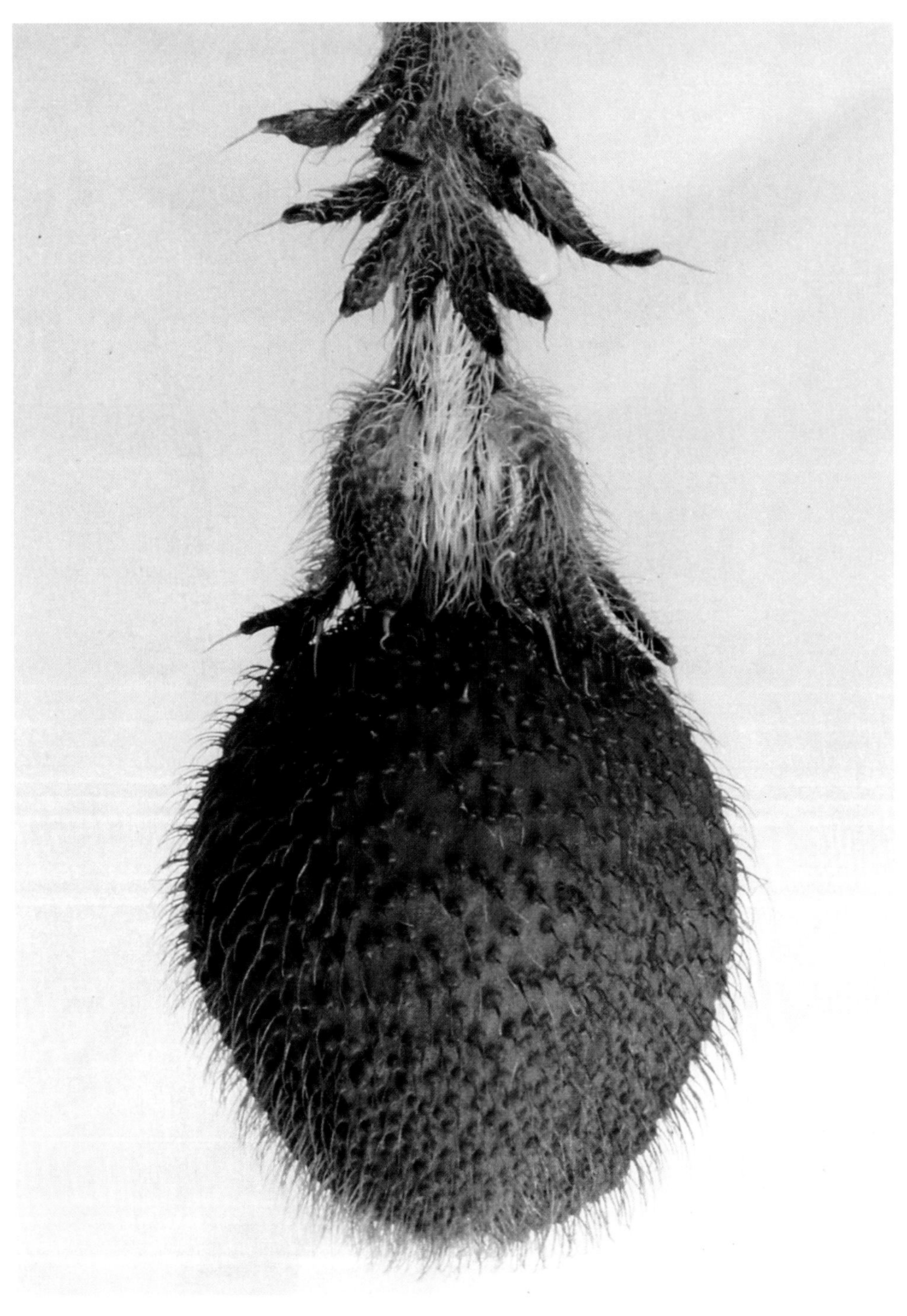

Despite all the geometry and symmetry, despite the character of
a classification book, all of a sudden something impenetrable,
something mysterious, comes through.
(Helmut Heissenbüttel, 1981)

Blumenbachia hieronymi (Loasaceae)
Closed seed capsule magnified 18 times

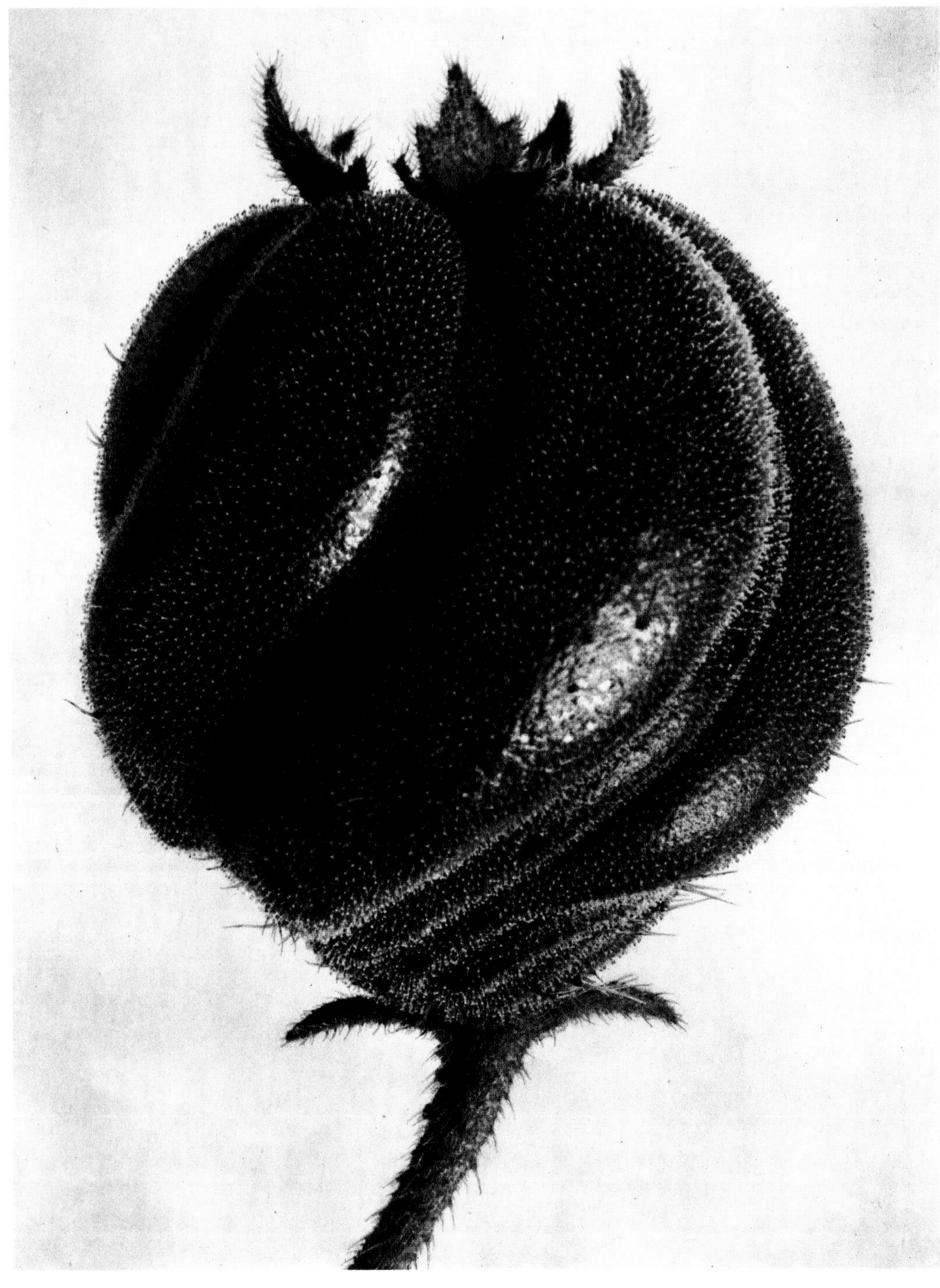

KARL BLOSSFELDT 1865–1932
LIFE AND WORK

1865 Karl Blossfeldt was born on June 13 in Schielo in the Harz Mountains, central Germany, where he also grows up. He attends a Realgymnasium (secondary school), where he takes the equivalent of O levels.

1881 Begins an apprenticeship as a caster in the art foundry of the ironworks in Mägdesprung in the Selke Valley and takes music lessons. Completion of cast-iron figures.

1884 A tradesman's scholarship in hand, Blossfeldt begins a drawing course on October 1 at the educational establishment of the Kunstgewerbemuseum in Berlin. His musical instruction continues.

1886 Blossfeldt completes his course, probably continuing with advanced classes at the same school. He possibly takes employment as an art caster.

1889 The drawing instructor Professor Moritz Meurer is commissioned by the Prussian Board of Trade (administering the Kunstgewerbeschule) to set up an effective and well-organized plan of study for drawing classes using nature as a model. This is to be the groundwork for the study of arts and crafts.

1890 In conjunction with Meurer's commission, six scholarships are awarded by the Prussian government to future teachers, two to modellers (Karl Blossfeldt being one of them), and four to artists (among them Max Seliger, the director of the Hochschule für Graphik und Buchkunst in Leipzig as of 1902). As assistants to Meurer, they are to collect material for botanical patterns, working around southern Europe using Rome as their base. Since Meurer is working with photographic samples which he made himself, it is conceivable that Blossfeldt begins systematically photographing plants at this time.

1896 Meurer returns to Germany; Blossfeldt remains a further year in Italy and considers emigrating to the USA.

1898 In October Karl Blossfeldt is made assistant to the director of the Kunstgewerbeschule, Ernst Ewald, where he gives lessons in drawing plants.

1899 Commencement of Blossfeldt's permanent instructorship at the same school, where he teaches "Modelling from Plants" for 31 years. He works with either natural samples or slides of his plant photographs projected onto the wall.

1910 Blossfeldt's second wife, Helene Wegener, is an opera and concert singer who accompanies him on numerous journeys. He uses the opportunity to continue his tireless efforts to collect and photograph plants.

1921 The Kunstgewerbeschule becomes a state university. Karl Blossfeldt is appointed professor, something which apparently has no effect on his subjects of instruction or syllabus.

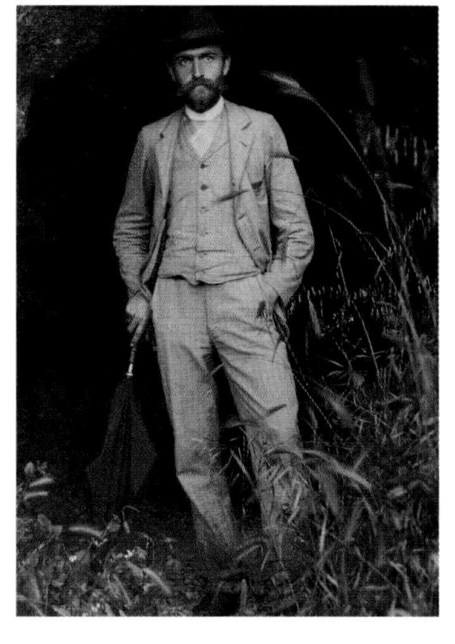

Karl Blossfeldt

1925 Sometime in this year the gallerist and impresario Karl Nierendorf assumes the management of Blossfeldt's plant photographs and promptly ensures their widespread distribution.

1926 First exhibition and publication of Blossfeldt's plant photographs outside of Meurer's art classes. The photos are published in periodicals and various books on architectural and design theory.

1928 First edition of "Urformen der Kunst", edited by Nierendorf and published by Wasmuth Verlag. Enthusiastic reviews in many newspapers and magazines lead to a second edition within a year. Wide acceptance amongst critics of Blossfeldt's work.

1930 Karl Blossfeldt becomes an emeritus professor of the university in Berlin and begins anew with the compilation of his plant archive. Commences work on his own theory of drawing.

1932 "Wundergarten der Natur" published in spring by the Deutscher Kunstverlag. The subtitle indicates that the book is a continuation of the earlier one. In a short essay, the only one ever to appear under Blossfeldt's name, the photographer provides a conservative estimation of his work and announces his intention to produce a design theory of his own. On December 3, 1932, Karl Blossfeldt dies in Berlin.

BIBLIOGRAPHY

Books by and about Karl Blossfeldt

Karl Nierendorf (ed.), Karl Blossfeldt, Urformen der Kunst, Berlin 1928, 1929, 1941, 1948, 1953, 1967. New edition with an epilogue by Ann and Jürgen Wilde, Dortmund 1982.

Karl Blossfeldt, Wundergarten der Natur, Neue Bilddokumente schöner Pflanzenformen, Berlin 1932.

Karl Blossfeldt, Wunder in der Natur, Bild-Dokumente schöner Pflanzenformen, with an introduction by Otto Dannenberg, Leipzig 1942.

Portfolio mit 12 Photographien by Karl Blossfeldt, with an introduction by Volker Kahmen, Cologne 1975.

Exhibition catalogue Karl Blossfeldt, Photographs 1900–1932, Bonn, Cologne 1976.

Karl Blossfeldt 1865–1932, Das fotografische Werk, with a text by Gert Mattenklott, botanical revisions by Harald Kilias, Munich 1981.

Exhibition catalogue Karl Blossfeldt, Pflanzenfotografien, with a text by Paul Wedepohl, Berlin 1984.

Andreas Hüneke, Gerhard Ihrke (eds.), Karl Blossfeldt, Fotografien zwischen Natur und Kunst, Leipzig 1990.

Ann und Jürgen Wilde (eds.), Karl Blossfeldt, Photographien, with a text by Gert Mattenklott, Schirmers Visuelle Bibliothek 23, Munich 1991.

A selection of books with illustrations by Karl Blossfeldt (with quoted reviews of his photographs)

Moritz Meurer, Die Ursprungsformen des griechischen Akanthusornaments und ihre natürlichen Vorbilder, special issue of Jahrbuch des Königl. Archäologischen Instituts, Berlin 1896.

Moritz Meurer, Meurers Pflanzenbilder, Ornamental verwerthbare Naturstudien für Architekten, Kunsthandwerker, Musterzeichner p.p., Dresden 1899.

Moritz Meurer, Vergleichende Formenlehre des Ornaments und der Pflanze, mit besonderer Berücksichtigung der Entwicklungsgeschichte der architektonischen Kunstformen, Dresden 1909.

Werner Lindner, Bauten der Technik. Ihre Form und Wirkung, Werkanlagen, Berlin 1927.

Das Deutsche Lichtbild 1930, Berlin 1929.

Karl Otten, Review of "Wundergarten der Natur", in: Schünemanns Monatshefte, Feb. 1929, pp.178-183.

Walter Benjamin, Review of "Urformen der Kunst", Neues von Blumen, in: W. Benjamin, Gesammelte Schriften III, Frankfurt/M. 1972, pp.151–153.

Stanislav Kubicki, no title (Review of Blossfeldts "Urformen"), in: a-z, Zeitschrift der Rheinischen Progressiven, Cologne, No.3, 1929.

Das Deutsche Lichtbild 1931, Berlin 1930.

Walter Benjamin, Kleine Geschichte der Photographie (1931), in: W. Benjamin, Das Kunstwerk im Zeitalter seiner technischen Reproduzierbarkeit, Frankfurt 1963, pp.67–94.

Das Deutsche Lichtbild 1933, Berlin 1932.

Das Deutsche Lichtbild 1935, Berlin 1934.

Fritz Kühn, Geschmiedetes Eisen, Berlin 1939.

Fritz Kühn, Sehen und Gestalten, Leipzig 1951.

Wolfgang Baier, Quellendarstellungen zur Geschichte der Fotografie, Halle/S. 1960, Munich 1977.

Otto Stelzer, Kunst und Fotografie, Munich 1966.

Helmut Gernsheim, Die Fotografie, Vienna, Berlin 1971.

Volker Kahmen, Fotografie als Kunst, Tübingen 1973.

Exhibition catalogue documenta VI, Vol. 2, Kassel 1977.

Helmut Heißenbüttel, Die Zeichen der Natur als Fotos, in: Süddeutsche Zeitung No. 209, Munich 12/13.9.1981.

Selection of books on plant photography (including sources of individual quotations)

Georg Christian Reuss, Pflanzenblätter im Naturdruck mit der botanischen Kunstsprache für die Blattformen, 7 vols., Stuttgart 1862–70.

Ernst Haeckel, Generelle Morphologie der Organismen, Allgemeine Grundzüge der organischen Formen-Wissenschaft, 2 vols., Berlin 1866.

August Corrodi, Studien zur Pflanzenornamentik, Leipzig 1876.

Karl Krumbholz, Das vegetabile Ornament, Dresden 1879.

Richard Hofmann, Blätter und Blumen für Flächen-Decoration, Vorlagensammlung für Zeichen-, Webe- und gewerbliche Fortbildungsschulen, Fabrikanten und Musterzeichner, Leipzig 1885.

Georg Wilhelm Aarland, Detail-Studien zur Malerei und Kunst, Photographische Aufnahmen nach der Natur, 5 vols., Leipzig 1887–1893.

Martin Gerlach, Blumen und Pflanzen zur Verwendung für kunstgewerbliche Dekorationsmotive und den Zeichenunterricht, Vienna 1892.

Ferdinand Luthmer, Blütenformen als Motive für Flachornamente, Berlin 1893.

Ferdinand Moser, Handbuch der Pflanzenornamentik, zugleich eine Sammlung von Einzelmotiven für Musterzeichner und Kunstgewerbetreibende, Leipzig 1893.

Jean Stauffacher, Pflanzenzeichnungen in natürlicher und stilisierter Darstellung, Breslau 1893.

Martin Gerlach, Formstudien, Fotografische Natur-Aufnahmen, Vienna 1895.

Ernst Haeckel, Kunstformen in der Natur, Leipzig, Vienna 1899.

Arnold Lyongrün, Neue freie Dekorationsmotive entwikkelt aus dem Tier- und Pflanzenreich. Eine Auswahl von Entwürfen im modernen Stil mit Rücksicht auf die praktische Verwendung im Kunstgewerbe, Leipzig 1899.

Heinrich Gross, Botanischer Formenschatz, Eine Sammlung von Naturstudien zur Belebung des Ornaments in Schule und Werkstatt, Stuttgart 1900.

Josef Ritter von Storck, Die Pflanze in der Kunst, Ein Vorlagenwerk für den Zeichenunterricht, Vienna 1900.

Wilhelm Weimar, Blumen-Aufnahmen, Nach der Natur fotografiert, Frankfurt/M. 1901.

Martin Gerlach, Formenwelt aus dem Naturreiche, Vienna 1903.

Roland Anheißer, Mikroskopische Kunstformen des Pflanzenreiches, Dresden 1904.

Richard Graul, Die Pflanze in ihrer dekorativen Verwertung, Leipzig 1904.

Richard Kieser, Das neuzeitliche Pflanzenornament, Wie entwickele ich mein Ornament aus der Pflanze, Krefeld 1904.

Max Seliger, Gutachterliche Berichte über eine sächsische Photographenschule, Leipzig 1904, Hauptstaatsarchiv Leipzig.

Wilhelm Weicher, Naturbilder, Aufnahmen aus dem Reiche der Natur, Berlin, Leipzig 1908.

Paul Dobe, Wilde Blumen der deutschen Flora, 103 Naturaufnahmen, Leipzig 1929.

Ernst Fuhrmann, Die Pflanze als Lebewesen, Eine Biographie in 200 Aufnahmen, Frankfurt/M. 1930.

Karl Otto Bartels, Blüte und Frucht im Leben der Bäume, 100 Aufnahmen mit einführendem Text, Königstein 1930.

Ernst Fuhrmann, Die Welt der Pflanze, Munich 1931.

Paul Wolff, Formen des Lebens, Botanische Lichtbildstudien, Königstein 1931.

Oskar Prochnow, Formenkunst der Natur, Berlin 1934.

Ernst Fuhrmann, Das Wunder der Pflanze, Berlin 1935.

Klaus Nissen, Die botanische Buchillustration, Ihre Geschichte und Bibliographie, 2 vols., Stuttgart 1951.

Georg Schmidt, Kunst und Naturform, Basle 1960.

Ernst Fuhrmann, Grundformen des Lebens, epilogue by Franz Jung, Darmstadt 1962.

Andreas Feininger, Die Sprache der Natur, Vienna, Düsseldorf 1966.

Nancy Newhall (ed.), Edward Weston, The Flame of Recognition, His photographs accompanied by excerpts from the daybooks and letters, Millerton NY 1975.

Wolfgang Kemp, "...einen wahrhaft bildenden Zeichenunterricht überall einzuführen", Zeichnen und Zeichenunterricht der Laien 1500–1870, Ein Handbuch, Frankfurt/M. 1979.

Exhibition catalogue Ernst Fuhrmann, Rolandseck, Berlin 1979.

Irving Penn, Flowers, New York 1980.

Rainer Wick, Bauhaus-Pädagogik, Cologne 1982.

Joel Meyerowitz, Wild Flowers, New York 1983.

Joan Fontcuberta, Herbarium, with a text by Vilém Flusser, Göttingen 1985.

Kathryn Kleinman, Sara Sylvin, On Flowers, San Francisco 1988.

Jürg Andermatt, Gras, Kiel 1989.

Oskar Bätschmann, Entfernung der Natur, Landschaftsmalerei 1750–1920, Cologne 1989.

Ursula Brecht, Freude mit Rosen, Weingarten 1989.

Yasuhiro Ishimoto, Hana, San Francisco 1989.

Exhibition catalogue Florence Henri, Avantgarde Photographer, San Francisco 1990.

Eliot Porter, James Gleick, Nature's Chaos, New York 1990.

Robert Mapplethorpe, Flowers, Farbphotographien 1980–1989, with a text by Patti Smith, Munich 1990.

Bec, Louis, Vorläufiger Versuch über die Upokrinomenologie oder: Eine verheerende zoosystematische Expedition durch ein Glossar, in: Florian Rötzer (ed.), Digitaler Schein, Ästhetik der elektronischen Medien, Frankfurt/M. 1991, pp. 397–416.

William A. Ewing, Flora Photographica, Masterpieces of Flower Photography from 1835 to the Present, London 1991.

Heinz Teufel, Bernd Küster, Monets Garten, Hamburg 1991.

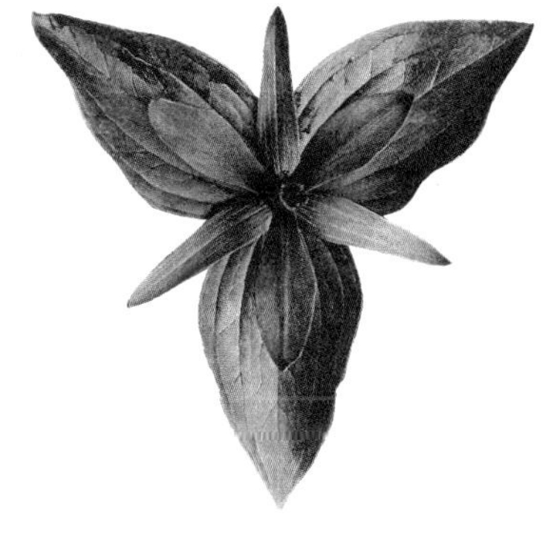

In this series:

- John J. Audubon
- Karl Blossfeldt
- Edward Burne-Jones
- Albrecht Dürer
- Feu d'Amour
- Wilhelm von Gloeden
- Kissing Animals
- Carl Larsson
- Matisse Cut-outs
- Carlo Mollino
- Alfons Mucha
- Naughty Paris
- Guglielmo Plüschow
- Mel Ramos
- Auguste Rodin
- Wheels and Curves